I CAUGHT A LITTLE, BIG FISH

To Kim –
On His Love –
Judy Briscoe Gorg

Lell Briscoe

I Caught a Little, Big Fish

Fishing for Faith
in the Heart of Your Child

Jill Briscoe
and
Judy Briscoe Golz

Servant Publications
Ann Arbor, Michigan

Vine Books is an imprint of Servant Publications especially
designed to serve evangelical Christians.

Unless otherwise noted, Scripture used in this work is taken
from the *New International Version* of the Bible, copyright
© 1978 by New York International Bible Society, used by
permission of Zondervan Bible publishers.

Published by Servant Publications
P.O. Box 8617
Ann Arbor, Michigan 48107

Cover design by Multnomah Graphics/Printing
Cover illustration by Krieg Barie
Text design by K. Kelly Bonar

94 95 96 97 98 10 9 8 7 6 5 4 3 2 1

Printed in the United States of America

ISBN 0-89283-827-2

Library of Congress Cataloging-in-Publication Data

Briscoe, Jill
    I caught a little, big fish : fishing for faith in the heart of your
child / Jill Briscoe and Judy Golz.
        194 p. cm.
    Includes bibliographical references.
    ISBN 0-89283-827-2
    1. Children—Conversion to Christianity. 2. Christian educa-
tion—Home training. 3. Christian education of children.
I. Golz, Judy, 1961–   . II. Title.
BV4925.B75   1994
248.8'45—dc20   93-49557

Dedicated to Drew and Jordan,
two terrific little, big fish
whom we love and thank God for
every day of our lives.

Contents

Introduction

∼

A COLLEAGUE WE WORKED WITH in a youth ministry once observed some young boys disrupting a meeting we were trying to lead. Seeing us grow impatient with them, he said quietly, "Hang in there, boys will be boys—but wait a while and boys will be men!"

It's vital to remember such wise counsel when our goal is to fulfill the words of Jesus: "From now on you will catch men" (Lk 5:10). Once we choose to follow Jesus, He puts a rod in our hand and directs us to rivers and lakes where He knows the fish are biting. All too often we think of fishing or evangelism as an organized church outreach, event, or crusade. We too seldom realize that the biggest fish can often be the littlest fish who haven't yet grown up to be big fish. What's more, they can be found right under our very nose. The little fish darting about our feet eventually grow up to be big fish. When you lead a child to Christ, you may well be "catching a little, big fish!"

This is a book about leading your children to Christ and keeping them Christian. After all, once someone is fished out of a sea of sin and landed safely on eternity's shore, they partake in a miracle. They turn from fish into fishermen. They receive a new nature and a new focus and find they now have the equipment in hand to catch their own "little, big fish."

But *all* fishermen need training, and it is the Christian parent's priceless privilege to provide some of it. This book tells a few of the lessons we have learned in God's fishing school. We hope some of the things we have learned (and are still discovering) will help and encourage those of you who are seeking to follow Him.

Judy Briscoe Golz
and Jill Briscoe

ONE

My father was a fisherman, and I am my father's daughter. My father was a "good" fisherman, but that didn't happen overnight. It takes time to learn the skills and become adept at the trade. Don't be too hard on yourself. Forgive yourself for "becoming."

~

Oh God, Make Me a Good Mother

Jill:

IT WAS JUNE 3, 1960, ten days after David Stanley Campbell Briscoe was born. Most mothers stayed a full ten days in the hospital in Britain before the great day dawned when they proudly carried their bundle of baby out into the real world. I had certainly never been so conscious of the bumps in the road, bellowing smoke stacks, or buzzing flies. We ran into my parents' house bearing our precious cargo of child—a child for whom I had become overwhelmingly, totally responsible.

I felt overcome, as if the weight of the entire world rested on my twenty-three-year-old shoulders. As I laid our baby on my own bed in the pink and white room that had been "mine" till I married, I began to panic. Now there were no starched white aprons around giving me a sense of knowledgeable authority or kind, informational medical types who seemed to know all there was to know about baby burps, moans, grimaces, and little mysterious night noises. David was eyeing me a little apprehensively, I thought—and with very good reason. It was as if he knew he was on his own... at the mercy of a total amateur, a novice, a clumsy, inexperienced nobody who had it in her power to make life wonderful—or miserable—for him.

I dropped to my knees in front of our firstborn and prayed a prayer my mother told me she prayed every day of her life: "Oh God, make me a good mother." David wriggled his tiny mouth as if to say, "I'll say *Amen* to that!" The great adventure had begun.

How glad I was to have my own dear mother on hand. Not that she interfered in any way, but just to have her there was a stabilizing delight. After all, she had walked this path twice before, making her the envied expert. I wondered what it was like for her to watch me. Having a child yourself is one thing; watching your daughter bear a child must be another.

Now fast forward to December 16, 1989, in the middle of a Chicago winter. Judy, my daughter, and I looked down at the precious bundle lying on her bed. Without saying a word, Judy looked at me. I could read so many emotions in her eyes—joy, thankfulness, peace, and apprehension. Suddenly I was back home in England seeing myself mirrored in Judy's wide but happy eyes. Almost thirty years after I had arrived home with my first baby, my daughter had arrived home with hers. Having a child yourself is one thing; watching your child have a child is another. I no longer needed to wonder what my own mother felt like—now I knew!

Judy:

Much later that night, I was too excited to sleep. Bringing a child into the world was the most wonderful and scary experience I had ever encountered. I looked over at Drew and thanked God for giving us a beautiful, healthy baby boy. But how was I going to rear him in this world? How was he going to learn to be the man that God wanted him to be? How would he withstand all the pressures that would impinge on him in our secularized society? All of a sudden I panicked. I had made a terrible mistake! I wasn't equipped to be a mother! I prayed, as Greg and I had prayed throughout the pregnancy, "Please, Lord, help us to be good parents. Help me to be a good mother." Feeling a sense of calm, I left my baby sleeping and went into the kitchen for something to drink.

Greg and I had just moved into this old house five days earlier, so boxes were everywhere. I grabbed a cup of coffee and retreated to the living room with Mom and Greg. I huddled under a blanket—the house was cold, and growing colder. Greg went down to the basement to try to figure out what was going on. When we bought the house, we were told that the furnace was old, but we had no idea that it would stop working. Greg's face was white when he came to break the news. He said he couldn't believe that on the first night in his life when he was truly responsible for a tiny human being, the furnace had died when the temperature outside was well below zero. Mom and I gathered as many blankets as we could find and wrapped them around Drew. Then, Drew, Mom and I got into our bed and tried to keep warm. In the meantime, Greg began the arduous task of trying to find a repairman to come out on this freezing night at 3:00 in the morning. Thankfully, he found an older gentleman who had been around when our ancient furnace was more popular. He fixed it so that it would get us through the night.

As Mom and I tried to keep Drew warm, I realized that so much can go wrong in this world, and we have no control over it. Yet, God is in control. He made sure we contacted the only man in our area who knew how to fix our particular furnace. This has been a good reminder to me in my mothering. We can prevent certain things from happening to our children and we should. However, there will be times when we will not be there or will be unable to protect them. We need to know that when we can't be there for them, God is. We need to teach them that they can always depend on an eternal being who loves them far more than we can ever love them. This is what I as a mother want to make sure my children know. If my children can grasp these ideas then I believe I have done the job that God has set before me. It's one way I can cooperate with God in my own prayer: "Oh God, please make me a good mother!" This prayer is not only my own, but it reflects the sentiment of my friends who are also rearing their children in this society.

Jill:

My heart goes out to Judy and her generation. "Tell me any way I can be sure my kids will make it spiritually," begs a mother of four lively youngsters. "Are there any sure-fire ways?" inquires her friend. I listen to my young companions and understand their concerns. As a mother of three and now a grandmother of six, I well remember wishing God would just lean out of heaven and shout, "Relax, Jill, they're going to be all right!" But He has never done that.

What God has done, however, is to tell me how I can know Him and trust Him for the wisdom to do my part in the equation. In the end, that's all we moms can do. We are, after all, fallen moms who have fallen kids. What do I mean by that? Perhaps you have an instant reaction to the mere suggestion that your children are less than perfect. My own mother was horrified at the very suggestion, believing (as all good grandmothers tend to do) that *her* grandchildren were "just right."

COULDN'T IT JUST BE SIN?

One day as I was up to my ears in nappies (English diapers), the doorbell rang. I hastily wrapped up my baby and pinned the nappy into place with a large diaper pin. As I picked David up and hurried to answer the doorbell, he began to howl. Jiggling him up and down did no good—in fact, the screams escalated. Dealing with the salesman at the door was difficult, but I sent him on his way and turned around to find my husband standing in the hallway looking on in consternation. By now David was purple in the face and into the "holding his breath at the top of the scream" syndrome. Stuart took him out of my arms, sat in an armchair, and bounced him furiously up and down.

"What's wrong with him?" he shouted above the howls.

"I don't know," I shouted back. "It's either wind, or he's hungry or he's got a dirty nappy—and I'm sure it's not that, because I've just changed him!"

"Couldn't it just be sin?" Stuart inquired quite seriously.

"Not our child," I assured him—though of course that

was certainly a possibility. As it turned out, the problem wasn't David's fallen nature making itself heard so much as it was the hurriedly placed large diaper pin that had impaled my son. But soon enough as we grew together, our family was to experience our fallenness making itself felt.

The problem is that all of us have inherited that part of Adam's nature that chose to be independent from God. The spiritual part of us isn't "just right," but rather "just wrong"! If we want to rear our children to know, love, and serve the Lord, we must take into account our inherited fallenness. As a mother, I have been convinced of my children's sin nature in a variety of ways.

The English game of bowls illustrates my conviction. The game is played on a manicured grass patch. A small white bowl, or jack, is rolled out first. Then people take turns trying to roll large black bowls as near as possible to the white bowl without hitting it. It sounds pretty simple until you realize each of the black bowls has a weight inside it pulling it off center! No matter how straight you aim these black bowls, they are bound to veer off to the right or to the left.

So it is with our children. We as parents know there is a godly standard (the white jack) that we try to aim at. We set off the black bowls (our kids) in as straight a line as possible, but that "off center weight"—the sin nature—insists on pulling them off course. Add to this the sin bias in our own natures, and parenting children becomes a monumental challenge.

"But this makes it harder than ever," wails a young friend. "We can't put that right, can we?"

"No," I replied, "but we can cooperate with a God who can put that right."

The challenge for us is to determine what the Bible says

about the principles and behavior of a Christian family. If, as the Bible teaches, "Children are an inheritance from the Lord" (Ps 127:3), how are we as parents to establish that heritage? This is especially complicated for those who don't have a Christian heritage, or who are single parents struggling to be both Dad and Mom.

I remember getting very jealous of Christians who gave their testimonies and began by saying, "I came from a long line of Christians (or missionaries or pastors)." *What must it be like,* I wondered, *to be brought up in a Christ-centered home?* Then one day a good friend listened to my jealous complaint about it and said brusquely, "OK—so you don't have a Christian heritage? Quit beefing about it and start one! You've made sure you've chosen a committed Christian spouse, now determine together that if God blesses you with kids, you will raise them to love and serve the Lord! And," she continued, "there are plenty of models in the Bible—start in the Old Testament. You'll find examples there!"

I took her word in season to heart and began to go to the Scriptures for help and instruction in these matters. It wasn't long before I met a wonderful mentor as far as mothering was concerned. I met my friend, Hannah, wife of Elkanah, and mother of Samuel. Her story is told in 1 Samuel 1:1-2:26 and forms the basis of this book.

Judy:

A WOMAN AFTER GOD'S OWN HEART

We'll be returning to the details of Hannah's story repeatedly throughout this book, but for now let us give you a thumbnail sketch of the challenges she faced.

Hannah lived in ancient Israel during the days when

polygamy was an accepted practice. Both she and a woman named Peninnah were married to Elkanah, a godly man from the hill country of Ephraim.

Year after year Elkanah and his two wives would go up to Shiloh to worship the Lord with sacrifices and offerings, and each year Elkanah would give to Hannah twice the sacrificial portions he gave to Peninnah. Why? First, Scripture says he did it because he deeply loved Hannah; and second, he did it because she was childless, while Peninnah had several children.

Hannah's agony over her barrenness was hard enough to bear, but her rival Peninnah made it worse by continually "provoking her in order to irritate her" (1 Sm 1:6). The cruel provocations grew especially severe at the time of the family's yearly sacrifice. "Whenever Hannah went up to the house of the LORD," says the Bible, "her rival provoked her till she wept and would not eat" (1 Sm 1:7).

In her despair, Hannah fled to the tabernacle at Shiloh and poured out her heart to God. She begged Him to open her womb and give her a son—a son she promised to "give... to the LORD for all the days of his life" (1 Sm 1:11). Eli, the high priest, saw her in great turmoil of soul and mistakenly concluded she had downed one too many! "How long will you keep on getting drunk?" he demanded of her. "Get rid of your wine" (1 Sm 1:14).

Hannah replied that she was not drunk but greatly distressed, and that she had been presenting an urgent request to the Lord. Eli sent her on her way with a blessing and Hannah returned home to her husband. Soon, God answered her prayer! In the course of time she became pregnant and gave birth to a son whom she named Samuel.

True to her word, Hannah reared her son in the fear of God. When he was fully weaned, she took him back to Eli

and announced that this son was the answer to her an-
guished prayer of a few years before. She then presented
Samuel to Eli for service in the tabernacle and joyfully
sang a beautiful hymn of praise to the Lord—a song that
Mary, the mother of Jesus, would echo many years later
when she visited her cousin Elizabeth to tell her about
God's miraculous work in her own life.

Hannah and Elkanah went home, leaving Samuel in the
care of Eli. Every year thereafter Hannah would return
and present her son with a little robe she had made. Eli
blessed Hannah and Elkanah for their faithfulness and
prayed that God would grant them other children "to take
the place of the one she prayed for and gave to the LORD"
(1 Sm 2:20). And the Lord did just that; the text says she
gave birth to three sons and two daughters. And on that
happy note, Hannah disappears from the pages of Scripture. From then on, her son takes center stage, becoming
one of the greatest prophets the nation Israel would ever
know.

There you have it—a thumbnail sketch of the life and
career of a godly mother who has much to teach us about
rearing our children to love and serve God. We don't
know much about Hannah, but what we do know pro-
vides us with a remarkable example of faith, courage, and
godliness. Her life embodied several principles that can
help us to become the kind of mothers we so urgently
desire to be.

Jill:
YOU ARE RESPONSIBLE FOR YOU

At the outset, there is one crucial principle arising out
of Hannah's life that Judy and I think should be made

unmistakably clear: *Mothers aren't ultimately responsible for their children's choices, nor are wives responsible for their husband's.*

Samuel had his own free will and needed to be responsible for his relationship to God, even as his mother had her own free will and was responsible for hers. God knows from His own experience that it is possible to bring up a son in paradise and still see that son go wrong. Remember Adam? God understands the Christian parent. He Himself wrestled with wayward, disobedient children who broke His heart, redeeming and restoring every one who would respond to His love.

But perhaps your concern is not your children but your husband. Perhaps someone reading these pages might say, "All this sounds fine, but my husband isn't even a Christian. What can I do when my partner's goals aren't remotely the same as mine? The things that are so important to me aren't important to him at all."

First and foremost, you must be concerned with your own accountability to God as a wife and mother. Leave your husband in God's hands! Hannah appears to have believed she was only responsible for *her* relationship with God—not her husband's. She did her best to do the things she believed the Lord was leading her to do without trying to manipulate her husband into doing the things she wanted *him* to do.

Pray for your husband and let him see the Lord in your life and in your mothering. And trust the God of Grace to open his eyes, melt his heart, and win your husband to Himself. You make your husband happy—God is the one who can make him good!

We don't mean to sugarcoat this. It's hard when you're

rearing children and one partner isn't a believer. But ask the Lord for wisdom and grace to put the principles you can into action... then leave it with the Lord. Be encouraged to know the Lord knows your situation exactly, is concerned, and wants to lend you the power to be what you should be for Him as a parent—regardless of your marriage circumstances.

HOPE IN GOD!

Is it really possible to rear children who love God despite their fallenness and the fallenness of the world? And if so, what are the steps to success?

Those are the questions we want to deal with in the rest of this book, but for now there are several things we can and must do. For a start, we can find biblical models to help us—Hannah, for example. I once heard someone say, "If you would raise a Samuel, be thyself a Hannah!"

That's the choice before us. Hannah made her choice to help her child love God and in so doing helped to shape the destiny of an entire nation. Of course, she didn't know that's what she was up to at the time! All she knew was that she loved the Lord and that she wanted to rear her son in a way that would encourage him to grow up loving that same God.

And we think that's a pretty worthy goal, don't you?

~

Dig a Little Deeper:

These ideas can be used for further thought and study—on your own or in a group.

Parents are not ultimately responsible for their children's choices. Wives are not ultimately responsible for their husband's choices. Each of us, however, is accountable to God for our own free choices.

Which choices?

- The choice to have a relationship with God which involves asking God to forgive us of our sin.
- The choice to care for that relationship.

Discuss

1. Write a thumbnail sketch of your life choices to date. Does that include choices having to do with God? If not, why not?
2. How can we create an environment where our children will find it comparatively easy to make Christian choices? List three practical ideas.
3. Read 1 Peter 3:1-7. What does it say to wives who can't make their husband's choices for them?
   What does the passage say to husbands (vs. 7)?
   What does it say to husbands and wives (vs. 7)?

Prayer

Praise God for giving us free choice.

Pray for people you know who are in danger of making bad choices.

Pray for wisdom and patience for women with unbelieving husbands. Pray that the men will come to know the Lord.

T W O

My father was a "focused" fisherman. Fishing was never far from his thoughts. During the long winter nights he would painstakingly make the flies that he would use to catch the trout he would chase up the rivers in the beautiful English Lake District. Even out of season he would be thinking, dreaming, and planning for those fishing trips. It takes a constant focus to make an effective fisherman.

～

A God-Centered Focus

Jill:

IT WAS 3:00 A.M. and I was fast asleep on the fourth floor of a hotel. Suddenly the fire alarm went off right over my head, catapulting me back to the real world. It took a while to realize what was happening. I turned on the bedside light and looked at the clock. I saw the hour and lay back on the pillow, waiting for the bell to quit. My ears were ringing so hard it almost hurt. I sniffed the air, trying to smell smoke—nothing. "Must be a false alarm," I said to myself.

After another ear-splitting minute had gone by, I got out of bed, put on my gown, and looked out the windows. I couldn't see any activity in the hotel parking lot beneath me, so I checked for the nearest fire exit, opened the door cautiously, and glanced out. Ten or so people were doing exactly the same thing.

"What do you think?" I shouted to a talking head.

"I don't know," the head shouted back.

"Maybe we'd better get out," advised a third person, as doors shut in unison. I closed mine and leaned against it, working through all the emotions engulfing me.

It seemed for real. If it was a false alarm they would have told us by now. I tried to call the desk but no one answered. That did it! *I'd better go,* I decided. I looked out my door and down the corridor again. People dressed only in nightwear were running down the long hallway toward the fire stairs. Everyone's arms were full of something. Some carried clothes; others held briefcases and files. A man hurried past with neither briefcase nor files— his arms were loaded with bottles of booze and under each of his arms sprouted yet another bottle. The strangest pair of wings ever! A young man lurched out of the door opposite me clutching his computer to his chest, while his wife struggled to keep up under the weight of her makeup cases and a pile of shopping packages.

As I turned to my own work of choosing what I must take with me, it occurred to me that I was witnessing a bonafide workshop on values. People had taken the things that meant the most to them. What was it the Lord Jesus Christ said? "For where your treasure is, there your heart will be also" (Mt 6:21). I glanced around the room, snatched up ten years of work in sermon notes in a black file, grabbed my Bible and purse, and ran for it!

There really was a fire. It was in the basement of the hotel. The fire engines put it out quite easily while half the residents stood around watching. It floored me that fully half of the occupants decided to stay put and watch the show out of their windows!

I wonder... what would you have taken with you had you been on the fourth floor of the hotel that night? What is more important to you than anything else? Answering that question may give you a clue as to your focus in life.

All of us have a focus whether we realize it or not. Our focus determines for us the direction and quality of our lives. It's absolutely crucial that we know what it is, and that we change it if we find it needs changing. Everything depends on our focus—a pattern, a philosophy of life that helps us to make choices in line with God's best for our lives.

Judy:

CHOICES HAVE CONSEQUENCES

We all have choices to make. We are perfectly at liberty to choose life or to choose death. We in the West value freedom as one of our greatest treasures, don't we? We are all free to act exactly as we please, without asking anyone. We cherish the right to live how we choose and choose how we live—but often we don't recognize that none of us has the right to choose the consequences of those choices. The people in the fire had a perfect right to choose to stay in their beds, but they had no power to dictate the results of their decision. If the fire had spread out of control, they would have been out of control, too. None of us rules our own destiny.

An increasingly individualistic society needs to hear the Christian perspective on this matter. It's hard to get people's eyes off of themselves and onto eternal issues, but I believe a "me-centered" world ends up sick of its me-centered obsession!

As Erma Bombeck so aptly puts it:

During the last year, I have dissected my marriage, examined my motives for buying, interpreted my fantasies, come to grips with mid-life, found inner peace, outer flab, charted my astrological stars, become my best and only friend. I have brought order to my life, meditated, given up guilt, adjusted to the new morality, and spent every living hour understanding me, interpreting me, and loving me. And—you know what? I am bored to death of me.

This struggle is a very old one. Many of the people in Jesus' day were focused on things other than the Master. Jesus provided answers for those people even as He does for us. In Matthew 6:19-34, for example, He describes some of the things that capture people's attention: earthly treasures, life, food, drink, and clothes. If we're honest, many of us would have to say that we, too, expend a lot of energy worrying about at least some of these items. Yet Jesus insists that we put our focus on Him and His kingdom, and He will take care of everything else. And He begins teaching us these lessons at a very young age!

When our family emigrated to the United States, I was allowed to bring two suitcases. One was for clothes and the other for toys. I had to decide which of my favorite toys I would take with me and which I would leave behind forever. For a nine-year-old, I had some tough decisions to make. Earthly treasures can become very important to us, and they did to me. I had quite a lot of stuffed animals and dolls that I was attached to, and yet they could not be packed easily. I realized right then that there was a cost to following Jesus. Even before my tenth birthday, I was beginning to learn that a sharp focus on God helps to shape every decision we make.

Jill:

Where do people go when they are tired of focusing exclusively on themselves? The smart ones look outward and upward where they may see God at work in people's hearts and lives and hear the good news that it's possible to receive the power to live by Him and for Him. The Bible is straightforward on this subject, proclaiming that God gave human beings a chance to choose life. We have the freedom to choose what God would have us choose or to reject what He would have us accept.

I well remember going on my own merry, wayward way without a serious thought in my head. I was eighteen and privileged to live in a wonderfully loving family that enjoyed the best things life offered in post-war Britain. My choices had been between tennis or skating, which boy to date, which movie to see, or what jeans to buy. I had my share of moral dilemmas but nothing that warranted too much concern or threatened serious consequences.

Then I went to college and the real decisions began. To work or not to work—that was the first question. I could complete my assignments honorably, or cut corners and cheat, using the time won to play. There were sexual choices offered to me, too, with much higher stakes than I had faced in a sheltered environment. There were religious choices as well. The most basic one was whether to be a religious "animal" or a secular one. Once one had chosen to be religious, the questions arose: How religious? And which religion to follow?

Along with a bewildering smorgasbord of religious offerings at college, I began to meet people who talked about Christianity. They told me about a man who claimed to be the only way to God, One who embodied truth and who offered the only viable option for life. And they invited me to choose life.

I knew that such a choice would force me to acknowledge that going my own way was the wrong way and that going God's way, revealed by Christ, was the right way. I had to be willing to be converted to Him. In other words, I was faced with the choice to turn around and head off in God's directed service. This I chose to do. I can only guess at the consequences in this life that would have followed had I rejected Christianity. I was not left to wonder about the eternal consequences.

I discovered I was perfectly free to choose eternal life or eternal death but not able to choose the outcome of my eternal choice. How thankful I was to become regenerated by the Spirit and to be assured of my salvation.

GOD AS FOCUS OF THE FAMILY

My choices continued as I grew in Christ. Would I marry or remain single? And if I were given the option, *whom* would I marry? Early on in my walk of faith I decided that if ever I had such an option, I would marry a man of God or not marry at all. Somehow I knew that my idealistic dreams of marriage and family must include the God factor. I knew that failure to include Him would leave my expectations hopelessly unfulfilled.

While by this time cracks were certainly beginning to show in the traditional view of home and family, traditional values nevertheless generally pertained. I can still remember writing college papers on the family with such quotes as, "The hope of civilization is the home and the hope of the home is the mother," or, "The beauty of a home and the strength of a home is that it is the product of affectionate cooperation and conspiracy between the prime participants of the contract." The home in this instance being comprised of a mom and a dad, three kids, and a dog. And who of my generation doesn't remember golden oldies such as, "The hand that rocks the cradle rules the world"?

Today we live in a very different world. Now we face the policy makers and leaders in our society who are struggling to come up with different definitions of family.

Judy:

A whole new set of choices have been presented to today's parents. For example:

According to Russell Chandler in his book *Racing toward 2001*,

> After culling a wide variety of sources, here's how Judith Waldrop and several other experts think home life will be redefined in the 21st century:
> —"By 2000, more than half of all children will spend part of their lives in single-parent homes.
> —"By 2010, about one in three married couples with children will have a stepchild or an adopted child.
> —"Most children will never know a time when their mothers did not work outside the home."[1]

The fastest-growing segment of homemakers in the twenty-first century will be unmarried men who live alone or head families.

Alternatives to marriage will be sought by older people as well as young singles.

Households now defined by the United States Census Bureau as "non-families" will eventually receive legal recognition as "families" in every state. Such arrangements will include unmarried heterosexual couples, homosexual couples, and friends who "intentionally" live together. (The current standard definition of what constitutes a family is a group of two or more persons related by birth, marriage, or adoption and residing together.)[2]

There will be increasing pressure to redefine "family" as "a group of people who love and care for each other."[3]

However, the principles we have taken from the story of Hannah and Samuel are applicable to all types of parents—single, step, or first married. Some principles may be more applicable at one point of family development than at another, but all are valuable and trustworthy.

A WOMAN WITH A FOCUS

Hannah was certainly a woman with a focus. She knew who she believed in and what she believed. Her faith gripped both her head and her heart. She lived out what she knew by putting her faith into action.

Don't make the mistake of thinking it was easier for Hannah in her day to determine what or who her focus should be than it is for us! She lived in a secular society similar in many respects to our own, a me-oriented and individualistic culture. In fact, the Bible says that in her day "everyone did that which was right in their own eyes" (Jgs 17:6)—not in the eyes of the Lord. Corruption was rampant even in the tabernacle, thanks to Eli's two sons, Hophni and Phinehas. Israel was economically disadvantaged and politically weak at this time in its history. Furthermore, "there is also a moral, theological dimension to Israel's trouble. Israel does not seem to have the capacity or the will to extricate itself from its troubles."[4] Yet, even in the midst of the corruption, sin, and weakness, Hannah sees past all of it and puts her faith in God.

Many people today may not be tempted by the allure of the secular world, yet they fall into the trap of being tempted within their very own homes by placing their spouses or children at the center of their lives. Family is important but not all-important. We mothers must make sure that we give our children all of the attention and provisions they need so that they can grow up to be responsible and adjusted adults. Yet it is a deadly error to make the family into God instead of allowing Him to be the God of the family.

Hannah knew her focus! Every year, Hannah, Elkanah, his other wife Peninnah, and Peninnah's children went up to the tabernacle at Shiloh to present sacrifices to God. Peninnah was obviously a very unhappy woman. She ridiculed Hannah for her infertility to such a degree that Hannah cried and refused to eat. Elkanah was distressed and asked Hannah what was the matter—wasn't he better to her than ten sons (1 Sm 1:8)? He may have been, but as important as Elkanah was to Hannah, he was not her personal focus.

You might be tempted to say that having a child was Hannah's personal focus. Yes, more than anything Hannah wanted a child. Could you blame her? In Hannah's culture bearing children was extremely important. In fact, "to be a wife without bearing children has always been regarded in the East, not only as a matter of regret, but as a reproach which could lead to divorce."[5] As she was constantly reminded by her rival Peninnah that she couldn't have a child, she wept bitterly. She prayed for a child and this was no ordinary prayer. Hannah tells Eli that she was "praying here out of my great anguish and grief" (1 Sm 1:16).

And, yet, what do we hear Hannah saying to God? God, if you give me a son, I promise to give him back to you. In that simple, powerful prayer, Hannah shows that her personal focus is God. Yes, she wants a son—a son who serves God.

God blessed Hannah and within time she gave birth to Samuel. After longing for so many years to bear a child, it must have been difficult for Hannah to fulfill her promise to God. Yet 1 Samuel 1:24 tells us that after Samuel was weaned, Hannah presented him to Eli to serve the Lord for his whole life. In Hannah's day, a child was weaned as late as age three or four. How hard it must have been for Hannah to let her preschooler go! My son, Drew, is three-and-a-half, and I can't imagine what it would feel like to send him permanently away from me at such a tender age.

In Hannah's case, it must have been doubly hard. Not only was she about to lose her boy, but she would be sending him into a place full of corruption. The sons of Eli the high priest "were wicked men," the text says, who "had no regard for the Lord" (1 Sm 2:12). They not only treated the holy sacrifices with contempt, they slept with the women who served at the tabernacle. I wonder if Hannah worried about the influences on her son's young life. Still, we don't notice any hesitation; she does exactly what she promised to do. She presents her son to be a servant of the Lord. I love 1 Samuel 1:28—"So now I give him to the LORD. For his whole life he will be given over to the LORD."

Hannah's example is extremely convicting to me. For while I haven't taken my children to a holy place and left them there to serve God, didn't I pray that God would make me a good mother? Didn't I pray that He would help me to make them all that they could be for Him? My children are only on loan to me and my husband for a little while. I need to make sure that I am giving my children to God for their whole lives. That's not easy! It means taking into account the possible consequences of that choice and beginning to pray about this even before the children are born.

Jill:

THE CHALLENGE OF PUTTING GOD FIRST

A short time ago I had the privilege of hearing a woman named Connie give a very moving testimony. She had parents like Elkanah and Hannah who loved and served the Lord. Because they believed the very best thing for everyone in their family was to be in the center of God's will, they asked Him where He would have them serve Him. Soon they followed His leading to Vietnam as missionaries. They believed with all their hearts that even though their children were exposed to an environment hostile to Christianity, this was the best possible place their little ones could learn about God. And God honored their faith!

When the Vietnam war began, some fellow missionaries were killed as the Vietcong overran their missionary complex. The little girl quickly found herself, her father, and her mother in the family car, desperately attempting to escape. The Vietcong stopped the car and ordered everyone out. Connie's father pleaded with the men. "Take me—let my family go." But God intervened and the soldiers told Connie's father to get back in the car and go on his way.

As Connie, now a grown woman with teenage children of her own, told that story, her eyes filled with tears. Not because fear of the memory overwhelmed her, or because anger at her parent's taking her to such a dangerous place distressed her, but because, like Samuel, she saw in her parents—and particularly in her father—self-giving love and sacrifice. It was in that moment when her father offered his life for hers that she, little, big fish that she was, caught her first glimpse of the self-giving love of God!

Connie's parents, like Hannah, had determined that as for them and their children, they would serve the Lord. If perchance this included running into problems, difficulties, and dangers, they would commit it to God and trust Him. Samuel grew up to love and serve the Lord. So did Connie. Following her parents' example, she served with her husband on the mission field and works today full-time in Christian relief work.

Judy:
WHAT ABOUT YOUR OWN FOCUS?

What is the personal focus of your life? What do you spend your time doing, thinking about, and worrying about? What types of things take up your physical, emotional, and spiritual energy? Sometimes it's difficult to determine the main focus of our lives because we have so many areas of focus. Our spouses, children, jobs, ministries, friends, and neighborhoods are all very important to us. Property, boats, cabins, sports equipment, furniture and collectibles can be too.

Every day the focus may change. Some things may take priority at different seasons of our lives. And yet, I think we have to ask ourselves the biggest question: are these things God to us, or is He the God of these things? Do we have a materialistic focus or a spiritual one? As one of Scott Wesley Brown's songs says, we must be in control of our things and never allow our things to control us.

Things upon the mantle,
things on every shelf,
things that others gave me,
things I gave myself.
Things I've stored in boxes
that don't mean much anymore,
old magazines and memories,
behind the attic door.

Things on hooks and hangers,
things on ropes and rings,
things I guard that blind me
to the pettiness of things.
Am I like the rich young ruler,
ruled by all I own?
If Jesus came and asked me,
could I leave them all alone?

Oh Lord, I look to heaven,
beyond the veil of time,

to gain eternal insight
that nothing's really mine—
And to only ask for daily bread
and all contentment brings,
to find freedom as Your servant—
in the midst of all these things.

For discarded in the junk yards,
rusting in the rain,
lie things that took the finest years—
of lifetimes to obtain.
And whistling through these tomb stones
the hollow breezes sing
a song of dreams surrendered
to the tyranny of things.[6]

Even Christians sometimes surrender their dreams to the "tyranny of things." Sadly, it seems all too easy for us to let our eyes slip from the Master to what is on the Master's table. Our focus shifts from the eternal to the temporal more quickly than we realize. But if we, as Hannah, determine to keep our eyes focused on the God of the universe, "things" will never get a death grip on our souls. As God remains at the center of our lives and our choices, we will be leading our children into fullness of life.

I was recently offered a very good job. I had just finished many years of schooling and was excited to finally enter the work force as a professional instead of being a graduate student. This job seemed perfect—I would be doing what I had trained to do, I had some expertise in the area, the hours seemed appropriate, and the commute wasn't bad. Still, an uneasiness tugged at me. Why did I find myself in such a tug-of-war over whether I should accept the position?

After many late nights discussing all of my options with Greg and praying about it, I decided that this job was not a priority for this season of my life. As the mother of preschool children, my priorities lay elsewhere. The job would have required me to cut back some of my ministries in order to have time for my family, my other job, and everything else. This was clearly unacceptable, as it would have usurped Christ as the focus of my life.

Jill:
GOD CAN TURN OUR WORLD AROUND

The Bible tells us our faith should be placed in God and our lives should be lived for Him. If we as parents can practice the principles of God's Word in our families, perhaps we can influence those around us. Moreover, it is not only possible to see our kids come to know, love, and serve the Lord, but it is God's great desire to assist us in such high goals and dreams. He will involve Himself in any family that will say to Him, "But as for me and my household, we will serve the LORD" (Jos 24:15). He will lend His power, peace, strength, and wisdom to the parenting process.

This does not for a moment mean that the forces of hell are not raging against the Christian family. We don't need to document the carnage in Christian leaders' marriages to prove our point—*but the carnage need not happen.* God is big enough and willing enough to lend us all that it takes to be God's people—and specifically God's women—in a hostile environment. We can be mothers who are a force to be reckoned with in our society. And God can turn our world around!

The early Christians were called "people who turned their world upside down" (Acts 17:6, KJV), but I would rather say they actually turned their world right side up! With hymnist Charles Wesley's "Right Man" on our side, "one little word from Him" will "fell" the devil and the people who propose his alternatives. Such a God is worthy of our undistracted focus, both now and forever!

Let me leave you with a question. Have you ever wondered how Hannah could sing a psalm immediately after giving her only little boy into the hands of Eli, Hophni, and Phinehas? It had to be that Hannah believed she was giving her child into the hands of God—and Eli, Hophni, and Phinehas just happened to be around at the time. Hannah undoubtedly believed that the safest place for young Samuel was in the temple which represented being in the center of God's will. Whatever trepidation she must have had, she was able to say, "My heart rejoices in the Lord."

And there is the key. Her heart was focused on God, fixed in His word, and filled with His Spirit. She could then in all honesty say, "My heart rejoices in the Lord" and *not* in my circumstances. To go home to Peninnah singing—even though she was childless again—must have taken all her resolve. But Hannah had made a promise to God and she was intent on keeping it. She had promised to bring Samuel up to know and love the Lord, as much as she was able, and this was the best way she knew to do it.

We are not called today to drop off our children at the church foyer into the hands of the pastoral staff. But most definitely we are called to follow Hannah's example in putting God squarely in the place He needs to be: the center of our lives. When God is our focus, the rest of our lives can't help but come into focus as well.

~

Dig a Little Deeper:

These ideas can be used for further thought and study on your own or in a group.

Discuss

1. Imagine you are on vacation. You have booked into a popular hotel. It is a high-rise building and you are on the fifth floor. The first night the fire alarm goes off just after midnight. You can smell smoke (you think) and know you need to get out. You glance around the room. You have no time to pack—voices are shouting, "Get out!" What one thing would you take?

2. On pages 39–40 Scott Wesley Brown talks about dreams surrendered to the tyranny of things. Write a paragraph explaining what you think this means.

3. Read Matthew 6:25-34 carefully. Jesus said, "For the pagans run after all these things" (vs. 32). Make a list of all the things Jesus mentioned.

   According to verse 32, is it wrong to need these sorts of things?
   Jesus sets out a main "focus" for His followers. What is it (vs. 33)? Put this verse in your own words.

Prayer

There is nothing wrong with possessing things. The problem comes when things possess us. Finding a right focus involves figuring out where your focus is at the moment. Spend some moments thinking about this. Ask God to show you where your treasure is for there will your heart be also!

THREE

I can remember following my father through thick, tangled undergrowth alongside the riverbanks. When we stopped to fish at a deep, still pool under a bent tree, I would watch my father cast his line. I would try and do exactly the same thing with my little rod. I'll never forget the day I caught a fish and my father didn't. There's no doubt about it, "more is caught than taught."

Jesus said, "Come after Me—and I will make you fishers of men!" We need to watch Him and do the same.

More Is Caught than Taught

Judy:

WHEN DREW WAS FIRST LEARNING TO TALK, he was in that wonderful exploratory stage of life. Any room he entered soon looked as if a cyclone had hit—pillows strewn across the floor, cupboard doors wide open, and contents of cupboards spread around the room. Unfortunately, the most frequent words that he would hear out of my mouth were, "Drew, that's a no-no." Whenever I said this, I would extend my right index finger and shake it back and forth. Pretty soon, Drew was walking around the house, shaking his finger at me and saying, "Mama, no-no."

As Drew began to speak more, we encouraged him to say please when he asked for something. I was having a difficult time figuring out why he wasn't "conditioned" to do this. Then one day I realized that when I was asking him to do something, I didn't always say please. Instead, I would insist that he do it. Once I started saying please, he quickly followed suit.

WE ARE MODELS

We have all encountered the importance of modeling in our culture. Young children usually identify with and imitate their parents. As the children grow older, they have a larger group of people with whom they interact, and therefore more choices for imitation. I am sobered by the power I have as a mother to model for my children. They imitate everything that I do—both the good and the not-so-good.

Whether we like it or not, we are models; the key is to be a good one! Hannah provided an excellent model of obedience to all who surrounded her. She kept her word and didn't go back on her promise to God even though she sure must have been tempted to. As she modeled obedience to God and kept Him at the center of her focus, her son watched and learned (even from afar). What a model Hannah is for all of us!

I wonder: How are we modeling the Christian life for our children? Can they tell by our behavior, words, gestures, attitudes, and values that Christ is the focus of our lives? If we want this for our children, then we have to be like Hannah and make sure that we have it for ourselves. In other words, if you want your children to be courteous and respectful, then you need to be courteous and respectful. If you want your children to have pure lips, then you need to have pure lips. You want your children to read the Bible—are you reading the Bible? If you want your children to know God, then you need to know God. My mother modeled this for my brothers and me.

One day when I was young, my mother was having her quiet time and my brothers and I were playing. Peter, my younger brother, needed to ask Mom a question. He found her in her bedroom and said to her, "I always know where to find you at this time of day—reading your Bible." Mom modeled consistency in her quiet time for us. Her example provided a huge incentive for us to mimic her spiritual disciplines.

When I reached school age, my parents gave me an allowance of fifty cents for cutting the grass, taking out the garbage, and feeding the dog. I'll never forget the day I earned my first allowance. My mom had put my allowance on the kitchen counter for me: nine nickels in a group and a tenth nickel off by itself. I remember asking, "Mom, why is this nickel over here all alone?" Her response was premeditated: "The first nickel is for Jesus. The rest is for you to use as you see fit." Giving me an allowance was a simple thing, but my parents took the time to use it as an opportunity to teach me a simple yet profound biblical principle. Until then, I had always assumed that what was given to me was mine.

Probably even more important, however, my parents modeled that principle. My parents viewed all that they were entrusted with as the Lord's. While not wealthy, they tithed consistently and were more than generous with what was left over. Most important, they obviously enjoyed the opportunity to participate financially in God's plan.

Greg and I have tried to model prayer and Bible reading for Drew and Jordan. One day I was hurriedly preparing dinner. Since the boys were very hungry, I began to feed them before Greg arrived home from work. When Greg came home, I gave him his meal. At this point, the boys were almost finished, Greg was starting, and I was trying to get my plate together. All of a sudden, Drew said, "Mom, we forgot to pray." I was embarrassed. In my haste, I had forgotten to thank God for the food. I was also happy, however. Drew had been the one who had remembered. He had seen prayer modeled for him and had remembered that we thank God for the food He has provided for us.

Our family also likes to read Bible stories. Even before Drew could talk, Greg would sit with him in the evenings and read to him. Drew has learned about the goodness and purity of Jesus from these stories. Unfortunately, however, his three-year-old mind cannot comprehend all that God is and all that we are not.

When Drew was potty-training, I used all the usual reinforcements—candy, other treats, and verbal affirmation. One day he did everything in the toilet he was supposed to. I told him that he was the best boy for running to the toilet when he thought he had to go. I went on and on about what a good boy he was. He then turned to me with a huge smile on his face and said, "Yes, I'm Jesus!"

GROWING UP WITH GOD

It's interesting for me as a mother and psychologist to see Drew develop. One of the things I am encouraged to see is the parallel development of his spiritual life with his emotional and physical being. Jesus is being integrated into his life as well as all of the other things he is learning about. He does not consider his spiritual being as separate from his emotional or physical being. Instead, they are integrated into a whole. He sees his parents trying to act in this way, and he does his best to imitate them.

Drew's brother, Jordan, is eighteen months old, a stage in life that consists primarily of wrecking anything Drew is playing with. Understandably, at times, Drew doesn't have a lot of patience with Jordan and tries to get him to stop. Sometimes the methods Drew uses are not appropriate however—such as pushing or hitting. When this happens, Jordan lets out a shriek. This is a practiced shriek and has become a consistent part of Jordan's vocabulary. If I am in the other room and can't see what's happening, I'll usually just yell, "Drew, stop it, leave your brother alone."

Now, every once in a while, Jordan shrieks for some other reason. Drew isn't even near him. Nevertheless, if I don't see what happened, Drew usually gets blamed. On one occasion when Drew had been falsely accused, I told Drew that I was very sorry. Then I asked, "Will you forgive me?" He responded, "No, but Jesus will."

Some things take a little longer to model than others! But the point is that Drew has learned that Jesus forgives others. Now he just needs to learn how to apply it.

Let me ask again: What are we modeling for our children? Is our focus visible in the environment in which our children are reared? From our earliest days, we were taught that our "family verse" was Joshua 24:15: "But as for me and my household, we will serve the LORD." Our parents made it clear that we as a family would share in God's service. It wouldn't be Dad traveling the world and ministering while we sat at home and did nothing. Instead, while he was gone, Mom bought a huge map of the world, and we would follow Dad's itinerary and pray for him.

The same was true for Mom. She wouldn't go ministering in the community without us. We became a part of whatever she did, for good or ill. When we were younger, for instance, Mom began a Christian preschool which we attended. She also decided to start a Bible study for the elderly ladies who lived in the area. Instead of merely calling the ladies on the telephone, Mom decided that it would be more meaningful if we personally went to invite them to come to the study. My brothers and I went with Mom to "help" her.

One of the ladies lived in a cute white cottage with a white picket fence surrounding the lawn. All along the fence, the lady had meticulously planted tulips about two inches apart. Everything looked so perfect. My Mom knocked on the door and the lady opened it. Cheerily, Mom described what she was trying to get started and asked the woman if she would be interested in attending. At about this time, a look of horror came over the lady's face. Mom didn't think the idea of a Bible study should evoke such a reaction, but then she realized what had happened. David, in trying to help make the lady feel good, had picked her tulips and was about to present them to her. He was saying, "Pretty flowers for a pretty lady." To no one's surprise, that lady didn't attend the study and we probably had been more of a hindrance than a help. But even early miscues like this ingrained in us the value and urgency of serving God.

Many people have asked me if I resented my parents' involvement in ministry. They wonder how I reacted to Dad's frequent travels. But resentment was never part of our experience; Mom and Dad practiced the philosophy that our family would serve God. They always included us kids, even if we didn't accompany our father on all his trips. We were with them—we were in ministry *together.*

Certainly there are those who resent their parents' ministry—some might have felt abandoned. We were not abandoned; we were included in everything they did. In fact, I have never known life to be any different than serving the Lord. God has always taken care of our family. And I firmly believe that if Christ is our focus, He will bless. I have never resented my parents' activity, but always thought it a privilege that God has chosen them to tell others about Him.

Still, one of the things we're called on to model is sacrifice. Do we know what it means to sacrifice for Jesus? Are we modeling selfishness or selflessness, giving until it hurts or grabbing until glutted? Sometimes God may ask us to put His kingdom ahead of the family, and this might mean that parents or children or even grandchildren might not all live in close proximity. Are we willing to model this kind of service for the Lord?

Hannah modeled sacrifice to everyone around her. She gave up her only son out of sheer obedience to God. And she did so joyfully!

Jill:

THE RESULTS OF MODELING

After Hannah had sung her song of praise, she and Elkanah returned home, and Samuel began to learn his trade. Now we begin to see the results of Hannah's remarkable modeling. The Bible says, "The boy Samuel worshiped the Lord there." The King James has it, the boy "ministered before the Lord under Eli the priest."

Immediately after detailing the sad story of Eli's wicked sons, Scripture records two wonderful words: BUT SAMUEL. It says, "... but Samuel was ministering before the LORD—a boy wearing a linen ephod." Ephods were long, sleeveless vests made of plain linen, worn by all priests. The little boy, well aware of those ministering to the devil (namely, Hophni and Phinehas), chose instead to minister to the Lord. The story of Samuel teaches us that good choices can be made by little people who have been reared by moms and dads committed to modeling a godly lifestyle. Samuel's new environment left much to be desired, but we should never discount the "God factor."

Eli was very old by now and his eyesight was failing, but Samuel appears to have kept close by his side and cared for him. Every year Elkanah and Hannah would visit the temple at Shiloh and Hannah would bring Samuel a little robe as a present. Eli prayed that God would bless Hannah for giving Samuel to the Lord's service and to him. God heard his prayers and during the next few years Hannah gave birth to three more sons and two daughters. As the psalmist says, "[God] settles the barren woman in her home as a happy mother of children" (Ps 113:9). "Meanwhile, the boy Samuel grew up in the presence of the LORD" (1 Sm 2:21). Many of us say we grew up in church, but Samuel wrote the book on it!

GROWING UP IN CHURCH

We can't expect our children to get excited about a church if we aren't involved and excited ourselves. And yet, there are people who drop their children off at the church steps and come back an hour later to pick them up. What are these parents modeling for their children?

My husband was very fortunate to have parents who loved and served God. His father kept a corner grocery store in a tiny seaside town in the north of England and he was also the lay pastor of a very small church. Stuart often jokes that he and his brother "were the Sunday School until we grew up and became the youth group!"

Every so often Dad and boys would set out to hold children's meetings in the small rural towns scattered over the beautiful English Lake District. Many of these hamlets had a church or chapel building but shared their pastor with other churches on the circuit. Stuart and Bernard helped to erect the meeting tent, pass out song books, and went with their father to visit homes and invite families to the meetings. At night they would pack everything up, heading for home and a busy week running the small grocery business in the small town of Millom. This, in a sense, was Stuart's Sunday School experience, and he always enjoyed being part of those rural outings.

There was no Sunday School experience for Stuart in his own assembly, but his devout parents conducted lively family Scripture lessons at home and instilled a conviction that church and Bible reading were not an option for God's children.

Unfortunately, the reality is we don't all live within walking or riding distance of a great evangelical church. Many of us can't find a fellowship with an attractive youth program for our kids. The temptation in that case is to stop attending church ourselves, do something at home, or do nothing at all. But we must do better than that.

When our family was very young, we lived in a country area with very few church options. Working at a vibrant youth center that already ran a Sunday worship service took care of some of the problem, but it wasn't "church." There was also a need for a Sunday School program for the children of the staff. I decided to obtain for us a local church experience and so started a Sunday School in our living room for our own children, as well as any un-churched youngsters from the neighborhood who could be persuaded to come along.

The Sunday School developed well and began at once to reach community families. I remember plunking Judy (three months) in the middle of our tiny living room floor and packing in the kids while David (two years) stood at the door welcoming people with a handshake and a bag of biscuits (cookies) for break time. That little venture opened endless chances to be invited into the farms and village cottages scattered around our youth center.

Every so often we'd have a "parents' open house." Since our little cottage was far too tiny for such an event, wealthy neighbors (not believers) made available their huge farmhouse kitchens and proud parents crowded in to see their kids dramatize or recite Scripture and sing Jesus songs. That's how I took care of the dearth of Sun-day School programs. Church, however, was a different matter.

Oh, there was no lack of church facilities. Beautiful church buildings dotted the verdant hills, including tiny ones hundreds of years old that the squire of the valley had built for his family to use for themselves, their share-croppers, and their servants. Some were a little larger, but while the stained glass windows and wonderful hand-carved pews were exceptionally beautiful, the people who used them were a dying breed.

The church in the nearest village was very old and very cold! A single heating pipe ran right down the middle of the building, but unfortunately the huge pillars that held up the roof ran all the way down the middle of the building as well. It was pretty discouraging for the vicar to climb up into his lofty pulpit and see not a soul, the handful of attendees obscured from his vision by the pillars. We were all sitting on top of the hot water pipes behind the pillars, trying to keep body and soul together. Every so often we would pop our heads out and smile at the vicar so he knew he wasn't talking to fresh air. All in all, however, it was very discouraging for him.

Despite the drawbacks, we decided to join the church and stick it out. We wanted to encourage the young minister, who was an evangelical and preached the Bible. He was new in our area, and when I heard he had come, I had asked an old lady who had attended the church for years what he was like.

"Well," she said hesitatingly, "he's a bit religious!"

Well now, I thought, *that's a change from the last one. We ought to go and support him.* And so we did.

MODELING FIDELITY TO TRUTH

Modeling church attendance is important, but equally important is finding a church where the pastor is a born-again believer who teaches Scripture and believes it to be the infallible Word of God. Hannah knew old Eli had his faults, but she also knew he was the best minister around. There was no Sunday School for little Samuel, but Hannah found a man who was a firm believer in God's revealed Word and said so. You'll never find a perfect church—and as Billy Graham has been quoted as saying, "If you find one, don't join it—you'll spoil it!" Churches are made up exclusively of sinners, so there are going to be problems. But church is still God's way.

Jesus attended His local church in Nazareth all his life. I don't know how alive that one was, or how interesting the village preachers. There were certainly lots of problems in His own congregation, but He still went. The first sermon Jesus ever preached, just after He began His ministry, made the congregation so mad the brethren tried to throw Him off a cliff (Lk 4:29). Yet Jesus continued to visit synagogues like His own and teach and preach there. It was His habit... and He wants it to be ours, too.

Our children benefited from the reverent atmosphere and the godly ritual of the church experience. It helped them sense the holiness of God. They learned to pray for the vicar too, that he wouldn't get fed up or so discouraged that he'd quit. David said once, "I wouldn't like to be the vicar when hardly anyone comes to church."

"Why, David," I answered, "every single person's important to God. When there are so few people it gives the vicar a chance to get to know each one of us. If there were dozens of people he wouldn't have time to spend laughing with us, asking you about school, or helping us with our problems."

As long as kids have something on their own level (and you may have to provide that for them yourself), a regular habit of churchgoing both models after Jesus and is a healthy thing to instill into your children from the earliest of days. And if the Bible is taught faithfully it is another regular way of learning the principles and practice of the Word of God.

WHAT IF THE KIDS DON'T WANT TO GO?

Unfortunately, it doesn't follow that just because you find a good church the children won't be bored. Did Samuel ever rebel? Did he ever run away from stuffy old Eli and his evil sons and find his way home to Hannah and Elkanah? Temple life doesn't seem to be too much of a life for a child. We don't know Samuel's thoughts or feelings, but it appears Hannah and Elkanah did some things right. Of course, none of us ever do it all right. But then, we never do it all wrong, either.

Hannah had such a short time to do what she wanted to do. If you and I knew we had four or five years with our child, what would we choose to make an essential part of their training? The early years are so important. Think of Moses. His mother had exactly the same opportunity as Hannah had—except Moses was being taken to Pharaoh's daughter to be brought up in a heathen palace. His early training was even more important than Samuel's. How did Hannah manage to instill such building blocks of belief into little Samuel? One thing we know for sure: she put God first and honored the temple as God's way of interacting with His people. She went to church and brought up her son to love it as well.

"But my kids are bored in church," complained a young mother. "Why should they go if they are bored?" Because, as my husband says so often, church isn't somewhere you go, it's something you are! Each one of us— man, woman, and child—are members of His body and should meet often for our Head's sake, not ours. Children can be helped to go to church with worship in mind, not self-centeredness.

But what do you do if your young Samuel doesn't

want to go—more, he *refuses* to go to church anymore? Samuel, it appears, had no option. There were some things that were nonnegotiable for him, such as Sabbath Day rests, feasts and festivals, and the like.

Even my husband went through stages where he was all but turned off to the local church, even though he was "all for Jesus Christ." In fact, he was in his twenties before someone called him on his attitude and asked him, "How can you be all for Jesus Christ and yet not be all for what Jesus Christ is all for?" That remark, his heritage, and other factors all combined to lead him into pastoring a local church—which at this point he has served as Senior Pastor for twenty-four years!

When our own kids were young, Stuart and I let it be known that there were certain nonnegotiable church events. For us it was Sunday morning services and special church get-togethers. It wasn't until Pete, our youngest, reached junior high that we had any problems.

It was young Pete who decided his dad preached too long and he knew as much (so he thought) as his Sunday School teacher. So he graduated himself from Sunday School and one memorable Sunday morning announced, "I'm not going to church—it's boring!" My immediate reaction was disbelief. He couldn't mean it. I put my foot in my voice and ordered him into the car. Judy, who was fifteen and very happily involved in church-related activities, gazed at her younger brother in total amazement. "You mean to say—I could have rebelled, too?!" she asked me. I was glad she seemed to think her opportunity was past.

I managed to get Pete to church but he disappeared behind the coatracks (the opposite direction of the sanctuary). I followed him behind the coats, trying to look as if I did this every week, and began a heated argument with my son. A lady suddenly appeared, taking a long time to hang up her coat. At last she asked me, "Have you read the Dobson books?" I was angry. Angry at her, angry at Pete for putting me in this position, and then angry at myself for being angry!

I suddenly realized I was more concerned about what the church thought of me because of Pete than I was about what Pete thought about the church. "Pete," I managed to say, "stay here if you must—we'll talk about this at home." I emerged from the coats aware of curious glances and left my son to decide if he would stay there or get himself into the service.

Over lunch we talked it out. Stuart told our son that while he was in our home, he would be in church. There was absolutely no option about that. Then he said, "But let's talk about Sunday nights. If you can give me good reasons not to go twice on a Sunday, I'll listen and be reasonable." By focusing Pete's attention away from the nonnegotiable option to a negotiable one, my husband won a battle. We also told him he would be in one youth activity a week, but he could choose which one. This worked as well. Pete chose not to return to Sunday School but to join a parachurch sports ministry—the Fellowship of Christian Athletes, which turned out to be a huge blessing in his life.

That reluctant young lad grew up to become a wonderful junior high pastor. What a heart he had for bored church kids like he had been. He designed puzzles and church service related bulletins to keep the kids' attention in church. Now he is Senior Pastor of his own congregation. Once more he has no option. Being in church is nonnegotiable.

TAKE TIME FOR TUNE-UPS

Models are a lot like pianos. Neither of them are much good if they're out of tune. So what do we need to do to be thoroughly in tune? First, we must have no known notes of discord in our spiritual lives. If our lives are "out of tune" and playing discordant music, we'll find our relationship with God affected. We'll need to ask the Lord to give us a spiritual tune-up to point out what's wrong and get our spiritual lives in order.

Second, we need to keep short accounts with God. Staying in tune means staying in touch on a moment by moment basis in our day-to-day schedules and not letting a heap of things pile up that we have to wade through in order to get in touch with God again.

Third, it's good to establish a time to meet with the Lord every day and even lay down some ground rules for yourself. Try to be honest when you are on your knees before God and promise Him that if He shows you something which needs to be dealt with, you'll try to take steps to do so.

It's frighteningly easy to get dulled to the sense of the Lord's presence. Remember, it took Eli a while to recognize what was happening to young Samuel.

That's why it's vital to do our best to keep spiritually fit every moment of every day. If the devil can catch us off guard, we might not even see a little, big fish nibbling at some bait. What a shame that would be. The most effective way to lead our children to Christ is to model a vibrant Christian life. The famous words of Deuteronomy 6 spring to mind. We are to talk to our children about the Lord "when you sit in your house, when you walk by the way, when you lie down, and when you rise up" (Dt 6:7,

NIV). That's modeling—day in, day out, in the car, out
of the car, at bedtime, mealtimes, and all times.

Judy:
WHEN MODELING PAYS OFF

Modeling a godly lifestyle can reap great rewards.
There's a lot of excitement when little, big fish get caught!
This is my story:

My mother was baking in the kitchen while I, at the
age of 4, was playing with my toys in the living room. I
had been hearing a lot about Jesus in my Sunday School
class and knew, with the limited knowledge of a four-year-
old, that to invite Him into my heart would mean that
some things would have to change. I approached my
mother in the kitchen and asked, "If I invite Jesus into my
heart, does that mean that I'll have to put away all of my
toys?" My mother responded, "Yes, Jesus would want
you to put them away." I thought about it for a few sec-
onds and said, "Ok, then I guess I won't," and walked
away. A few minutes later, however, I came back and said,
"Even if I have to put away the toys, I want Jesus in my
heart." Without even wiping the flour off her hands, my
mom knelt with me by the couch in our living room and I
accepted Jesus as my personal Savior.

This experience taught me a few lessons. First, Mom
has admitted to me that she struggled, even if only for a
moment, about how to answer my question about the
toys. Everything in her mother heart wanted me to invite
Jesus into my heart then and there, and deal later with the
hard issues of the Christian life. Yet, she knew that this
wouldn't be honest and wouldn't represent what Christ

expected of me. Mom taught me by her words and her actions that becoming a Christian would mean my life would be different. Jesus would want me to try to live up to His standards through the power and presence of His indwelling Spirit, and not the standards of this world.

Second, when I said I wouldn't invite Jesus in and walked away, she let me go. Now that I'm a mother, I know how difficult that must have been for her. She has since told me that she prayed and relied on the Lord to show Himself to me—just one example of my mother's prayer life. For many years I have had the privilege of watching and learning how to pray from my mom. She has taught me that sometimes we need to realize that doing or saying something may be the worst thing we can do in a given situation. Instead, we need to pray that the Lord's will would be done and that He would guide us and the people involved.

Finally, this experience taught me that our family is our first mission field. Although Mom was busy running a nursery school, working with street kids, and rearing my brothers and me, she lived every day of her life believing that the ground beneath her feet was holy ground. Wherever God had placed her that day was her mission field, and she should show His love to those around her.

On that particular day, she realized how important it was to explain God's truths to me. Now that I'm a mother of young children, this lesson has become especially significant to me. Sometimes, amidst the never-ending loads of laundry and the continual tidying and cleaning of the house, I forget that the ground beneath my feet is holy. God has placed me here for a purpose. I need to be His servant and minister to my children.

Jill:

HOLY GROUND

We parents will be ready for the wonderful privilege of leading our children to Christ as soon as we get hold of the concept that any time our feet and God's feet are standing on the same piece of ground, that piece of real estate is "holy ground." I think back to those early days when our kids were young. My husband's frequent travels militated against my staying in touch with God. As a young wife and mom I missed him dreadfully. I struggled with resentment against the mission we served which asked him to do so much traveling. Self-pity clothed my spirit most of the day and I experienced bouts of anger at God for putting us in this particular place of service. It wasn't fair!

My problem was similar to that of a young woman who heard my husband speak many years ago at some meetings in Belgium. During the course of the convention this obviously unhappy missionary wife came to talk to him. She was disgruntled with the mission, with her husband, and with God. She told my husband, "I feel like my three-year-old. When I take him to church, he wriggles and fiddles and won't sit still. The other Sunday I kept telling him to sit down. In the end he reluctantly complied. After a minute he whispered to me, 'Mommy, I'm sitting down on the outside, but I'm standing up on the inside!'"

"That's just like me," the young woman finished, tears streaming down her face. "I'm no good to God, my family, or even to myself like this."

Stuart was able to pray with that sweet young lady, who

chose to respond to his counsel by "sitting down on the inside" to the will of God. What a transformation occurred! Our families kept in touch, and we heard of blessings flowing from her mother heart that reached not only her own children but many other families as well.

My own battle ended in a similar fashion. In time I realized I needed to accept a period of privation as God's will for us as a family at that particular time and in that particular place. Eventually I grew sick of being sick about it. I battled it out with the Lord, and He won. It would have done no good just to give in to God and snarl, "Oh, all right—have Your own way, if You must."

When I came through to real acceptance of my own difficult circumstances, God began to use my family situation in a redemptive way. I began to buy back the opportunities that only this particular situation afforded me. One of those unique opportunities was to lead two of our "little, big fish" to Christ. Had I not come to a point of submission and glad acceptance of His will for our family, I would not have been in touch with God on those two occasions when Judy and Peter came to Christ. Because I'd made my peace with God, my heightened awareness of eternal realities helped me to be ready for the inestimable privilege of seeing my kids into the kingdom!

May I gently ask—is there anything that needs settling between yourself and God? Let me encourage you to put things right as quickly as you can. Don't miss being a mom with her feet firmly planted on holy ground when your children hear the Lord calling their names.

Dig a Little Deeper:

These ideas can be used for further thought and study on your own or in a group.

Discuss

1. Read the following thumbnail sketches of mothers. Name one thing each is modeling.
   - Moses' mother—Exodus 2:1-3 and Hebrews 11:23
   - Ruth—Ruth 4:13-16
   - The widow—2 Kings 4:1-7
   - The Canaanite woman—Matthew 15:21-28

2. The fact that you model something doesn't necessarily mean your children will catch it, but there is something that suggests it can happen. Read 2 Timothy 3:5. What strikes you about this verse?

3. Because we are born with a sinful nature, there is no such thing as a perfect mother. But there is such a thing as an imperfect mother with a perfect God living inside her! Proverbs 31 gives us a picture of a woman who is a model (fortunately she never existed, so we don't have to go on a guilt trip) of motherly perfection.

   Read Proverbs 31:10-31 and make a list of the reasons her children called her "blessed" (vs. 28).

Prayer

Pray that our churches will teach biblical principles of marriage and family.
Pray for Christian parents you know.
Pray for yourself as a parent.

F O U R

It was wartime and my father was home on leave. The world was in crisis. My father was stressed out. We took a day's fishing trip to the English lakes. I could see Father's face visibly relax. "It's good to get your mind off your worries and onto the things that really matter!" he said.

~

Parenting in the Midst of Crisis

~

Jill:

STUART AND I WERE in Northern Ireland at the beginning of "the troubles," as the folks over there call the war with the Irish Republican Army. We had been invited by Bill, a friend of ours and a prominent Irish businessman, to speak at some youth meetings in the city. It was exciting and not a little dangerous to attempt to hold a Youth Crusade in an area where bombs regularly exploded.

The last day of the crusade we were having a meal in a restaurant with our friends when a policeman walked up to our table. "I'm sorry to tell you the I.R.A. has placed forty bombs in your business tower and all that's left is rubble!" he said.

Our friend's offices were in a high-rise business area in

the center of the city. We accompanied the policeman, serenaded by sirens and fire engines, and soon found ourselves standing in the ashes of Bill's life. Several others were there too—scores of people shared that business complex. One man snapped at Bill as he walked past us, "Tell me how you cope with this! Some sort of a God who'd let this happen to us." As the man disappeared, Bill whispered to us, "He's a believer."

The fire chief came up to our friend and said, "I'm so sorry. We all know you are a Christian man trying to work for reconciliation between Catholic and Protestant. We respect you for all you do. We'll do our best to work all night to see if we can salvage anything for you." We all looked at Bill as he put his hands kindly on the fire chief's shoulder and said, "I don't want you to do that, my friend. Tomorrow is the Lord's day, and we should all get some rest so we can be fresh to worship Him."

Here were two men, both believers. One blamed God and let his trouble drive him from God. The other took "the spoiling of his goods cheerfully" (Heb 10:34, NKJV) and let the same trouble drive him into the arms of God.

CRISIS AND CHOICE

None of us escape this life without facing a number of crises. They come without permission or warning. It's how we respond to these crises that determines the sort of families we will produce.

Hannah is a classic example of how to deal with crisis in a godly way. And the greatest crisis of her life occurred before she even had children. The same crisis she faced is all too familiar to a growing number of families today—the crisis of infertility.

Judy:

It may be that nothing brings so much pain for a woman as the pain of infertility. One woman struggling with her own childlessness summarized her feelings this way: "My infertility is a blow to my self-esteem, a violation of my privacy, an assault on my sexuality, a final exam on my ability to cope, an affront to my sense of justice, a painful reminder that nothing can be taken for granted. My infertility is a break in the continuity of life. It is, above all, a wound—to my body, to my psyche, to my soul."

Those suffering from infertility often feel and think along similar lines. Researchers have found that depression, despair, and hopelessness frequently plague infertile women, along with a profound sense of loss. Health, self-esteem, self-confidence, security, status, control, and relationships often suffer. Many infertile people become angry. They may express feelings of inadequacy, incompleteness, loneliness, sadness, guilt, shame, frustration, grief, hope punctuated by disappointment every month, and jealousy toward women able to bear children.

Jill:

Hannah knew well the heartbreaking cluster of emotions associated with childlessness. The Scripture describes the physical state of her womb as barren (1 Sm 1:2), but it could very well describe the emotional state of her spirit as well. The Bible tells us she was in great pain. Perhaps the pain of longing to have a child is the sharpest pain of all. Today incredible advances in medical technology help infertile couples to conceive. Hannah had no such modern medical miracle at hand. The endless wondering why her hungry womb was empty must have only added to her self-recriminations: "Is it my fault?"

Listen to how her feelings are set out in the Scriptures. "She wept and would not eat" (vs. 7); she was "down-hearted" (vs. 8); she was in "bitterness of soul" and "wept much" (vs. 10); and she was "in misery" (vs. 11). She describes herself as "deeply troubled" and pouring out her soul to the Lord (vs. 15); and "praying here out of my great anguish and grief" (vs. 16). Infertility does that to a person.

RELATIONAL AND SPIRITUAL PAIN

Emotional pain was just the start of Hannah's troubles. The scourge of relational pain followed close behind. Those of us who are married to one husband and who have him all to ourselves can hardly imagine the conflicts rife in Hannah's home.

Just imagine sharing your husband with a rival. "Oh," some of you answer, "I know just what that feels like. My husband left me for another woman." But imagine if he hadn't left you, if in fact he had moved the other woman right in along with you. Then imagine him having a brood of children with her. Think of him growing tired of her but refusing to put her out of the house! Suppose he were to come back to you and made it clear that you had regained first place in his life. Imagine on top of all of this that you were infertile but with no alternative other than to live in a tiny house with lots of kids belonging to your rival. Then add to this the growing bitterness and anger of the other woman, who tried to assuage her own anguish by taunting you about your infertility—and no doubt telling you to keep your hands off her kids! How would you feel? It's hard to imagine, but try. Pretty awful, I should think.

The Bible says Peninnah was provoking Hannah relentlessly because the Lord had closed up her womb (1 Sm 1:6). Certainly, this was a pretty low thing to do—but we have to remember, Peninnah was a desperately unhappy lady too.

I think the hardest thing Hannah was forced to bear, however, were the words Peninnah threw at her about the Lord. "The Lord has closed your womb!" she spat at Hannah. This caused Hannah enormous misery—great spiritual pain. What had she done? What sin had she committed for God to punish her in such a fashion? And how could she prove her rival wrong? She couldn't, so long as she remained childless.

And so Hannah was forced to deal with the unholy trinity of emotional pain, relational pain, and worst of all, spiritual pain.

SHENANIGANS IN SHILOH

Where could Hannah turn? Where could she go? Emotionally, she was distraught and there weren't any psychologists to help her deal with her feelings. Neither did she have the support of her family or friends. Peninnah certainly had no interest in becoming a positive source of support, and even kind Elkanah couldn't quite understand what Hannah was going through. He just didn't know the right words to say.

Could she have gotten on the phone and called her pastor? And what about the church? What were the "Christians" doing to help?

As you know, that was another ungodly mess! The only priests that Hannah could turn to were Eli and his two worthless sons, Hophni and Phinehas; and the only church was plagued with scandal (1 Sm 2:12).

We get a clue why things were in such bad shape in the temple at Shiloh in 1 Samuel 2:27-30. A man of God confronted Eli about goings-on in the temple. He reminded the old priest that he had enjoyed a godly heritage; that God had chosen Eli's father out of all the tribes of Israel to be His priest (vs. 28); but that Eli had disdained and discarded the privileges of his past.

People who made sacrifices in the temple at Shiloh did so in order to have their sins forgiven. Eli's sons, however, were stealing the offerings and making fun of the people's repentance. God could not possibly allow this to continue and was about to bring judgment on Eli and his sons. Eli was to be judged because the old priest honored his sons more than God (1 Sm 2:15, 29), not only by refusing to control their behavior and by turning a blind eye to their promiscuous affairs with the women helpers in the temple, but because he himself indulged himself with stolen meat from the offerings his boys had torn out of the hands of the would-be worshipers (1 Sm 2:12-16)!

This was not the sort of situation in which people in trouble would like to find themselves, yet these men were the head of the only church Hannah had. When Hannah was praying fervently, her heart breaking, Eli thought she was drunk. Just how far out of touch can a man of God get?

When you collect all the facts about the spiritual counselors available to Hannah, it looks pretty grim. First Samuel 2:12 tells us Eli's boys were "sons of Belial" (KJV), "wicked men" (NIV), "evil men" (TLB). They had chosen to serve the devil, not the Lord. They "had no regard for the Lord" (NIV), "did not love the Lord" (TLB), "knew not the Lord" (KJV). They were thieves (vss. 13-17) and adulterers (vs. 22) and their sin was "very great" in the eyes of the Lord (vs. 17). Eli, the Bible says, was now very old, but well aware of what was going on. He knew that his sons were seducing the young women who assisted at the entrance of the tabernacle, but they wouldn't listen to his mild rebukes. He gave up trying to restrain them (1 Sm 2:25, TLB).

Who were these young women? They were holy women who had devoted themselves to tabernacle service, relinquishing all worldly connections and home life to do it. At least, they were holy women until Hophni and Phinehas got to them!

HELP IN TIME OF CRISIS

When you are going through deep waters and turn to the church for help, you expect to find it. If you don't, or find worse things happening in the church than are going on outside of it, you can feel pretty alone in a big cold, cruel world. That's exactly how Hannah must have felt.

Do you ever feel there's nowhere to go? That for good reasons you can't share your pain with the people nearest to you? That in fact the people nearest you are the very ones inflicting the deepest wounds? And have you in your extremity ever turned to the church and found deep disillusionment instead of help and healing? Then you know how Hannah felt. *Yet she did not allow that to turn her away either from the Lord or His people.* Had she done so, her crisis never would have found resolution.

Today there is a growing cynicism about the church. Leaders are falling into sin like skittles. Prominent Christian "stars" are plummeting to earth and many parents who in the past would look to their church leaders to lend a hand in rearing their children in a Christian way are thinking again.

We need to remember that the church of Jesus Christ is made up exclusively of sinners. It is a bunch of "being made like Jesus" people. We need to think what these folk would be like if they didn't know the Lord at all. This is not to say that Christians and their leaders should be allowed to live any old way and do any old thing. Of course not. But there will be all sorts of people within the body of Christ who are at many different levels of Christian experience. If we expect perfection, we shall surely be disillusioned.

Hannah dealt with her crisis by finding the best thing she could and sticking with it. Eventually that is where she found her answer. And no doubt she spent much of her time praying for the leaders at the temple.

LET YOUR TROUBLE DRIVE YOU TO GOD

Hannah found herself in an unenviable position, yet she found a way to get her circumstances to work for her rather than against her. First, she allowed her trouble to drive her to God and not away from Him. So often when we are in pain, we turn away from our only source of help. It's so easy to shake our fists in the face of a seemingly inactive God and blame Him. But we don't get a hint of that in Hannah's attitude.

Second, Hannah could have turned on her tormentor,

Peninnah, but she didn't. The Bible records no words of vindictiveness or recrimination. It would have been easy for Hannah to try to find someone other than God to blame, seeing Elkanah favored her and probably would not have rebuked her for sounding off. But God was her judge and she submitted herself to the One who could see the motives of human hearts.

Third, Hannah allowed the whole situation to produce sterling character in her. Hannah didn't give up. It's usually true that living in faith with an ongoing problem tends to produce endurance that at the end of the day translates into Christian character. Living with disapproval is one of those experiences that gives us a daily workshop, a chance to grow, as I discovered when our family first traveled to America.

We were so eager to show off all the exciting things we had been discovering. We wanted our loved ones in England to come and visit us. I even wanted my mother-in-law to come! Mother and I had a moderately good relationship (as long as we weren't around each other too much), but our backgrounds were vastly different and there were some things about my way of life that she just didn't like. In other words, she disapproved. While we could visit for a few hours it was fine. Now we had invited her to come and stay for three whole months. I began to wonder how it would all pan out.

Mother came and we had a great time. I was foolish to be concerned, I told myself. But then she was diagnosed with cancer and we faced some big decisions. Seeing there was no close relative left in England to care for her, it didn't take long to decide she would stay with us till the end. Now she and I needed to get along together. It wasn't going to be easy.

Pain exasperated the situation and as I struggled to be "all things to all men" (I was a busy mom to three, pastor's wife to a burgeoning church, and now caregiver to my mother-in-law), my disapproval rating rose. Both of us were struggling.

I went through an internal battle. I began by blaming God. "Why did You let her visit at this particular time?" I demanded. "You knew she had cancer." I blamed Mother for her attitude. I was trying my level best to do it all right—it wasn't fair she disapproved. Then I got around to blaming myself. I began to wonder if she was right to disapprove. Perhaps I was at fault here and there and I should be doing better.

At last, I figured out what was happening. I got around to owning what I needed to own (which was quite a lot, as it turned out). I said I was sorry and as far as it depended on ME, set about making my peace with her. That brought a lot of release and opened me up to a new relationship with God, my husband, and my mother-in-law. In turn, she was able to tell me her heart, and God defused an explosive situation and brought us together instead. Much more than that, I was even able to thank God for the character-building experience, realizing that He in His strange, permissive will allows us to go through tough times in order to prove Him present, powerful, and faithful.

That experience did a lot for my faith. Like Hannah, I learned to live with a less-than-ideal situation, thanking God in advance for what He was going to do in His sovereign will for His glory and the ultimate good of His children. I also learned that even when our personal focus is God, we often get tested on it. Like Job, it's good to be able to truthfully say, "When he has tested me, I will come forth as gold" (Jb 23:10).

Judy:

How do you handle the crises that blow into your life? How does your handling of those difficulties shape your children's perception of God and their willingness to trust Him with their very lives? Hannah is a terrific model for me in how to handle a crisis in a way that honors God. Many of us would not have handled Hannah's situation nearly as well as she did. Sometimes, when we are criticized, we lash out because we have been hurt. Or, we may withdraw and decide to shield ourselves from being hurt again. Learning how to deal with criticism appropriately can be a key skill in dealing with crisis. Paul has some wise words about how to deal with criticism in 1 Corinthians 4:3-5:

> I care very little if I am judged by you or by any human court; indeed, I do not even judge myself. My conscience is clear, but that does not make me innocent. It is the LORD who judges me. Therefore judge nothing before the appointed time; wait till the LORD comes. He will bring to light what is hidden in darkness and will expose the motives of men's hearts. At that time each will receive his praise from God.

Jill:

In verse 3, Paul said he cared only a little that he was judged. He didn't say that he didn't care at all, that it was nothing, or that it didn't bother him. But he didn't allow the criticism to become all-consuming. When you think about the things for which you are criticized, can you try to be objective and think if any of it might be true? If so, then "own" and "fix" what you can and don't dwell on the rest.

Let me illustrate what I mean by owning what you can. I remember being taken out to lunch by a girl who wanted to talk to me about Bible teaching. She told me she thought my lessons were shallow and lacked biblical depth. She also asked me how my quiet times were going —a question that told me she obviously didn't believe I was having one!

I remember being irritated and not a little hurt. Self-justification jumped up to say something, but I was able to resist the words and listen to what she was saying instead. I knew I had to apply 1 Corinthians 4 to my reaction. I prayed that the girl's criticism would not consume me. I asked the Lord to make me objective and help me own what I needed to own.

In the end I was able to say, "You know, I'm sure you are right. In some ways I am shallow and lack depth, and that is possibly why my talks struck you as superficial. I need to grow in God as all of us do. Pray for me." She was startled, but went on to say that she thought I shouldn't be teaching until I was "deeper." This I was able to leave alone—I knew that God wanted me teaching. Anyway, in the research for my lessons I was growing deeper and deeper in the Lord. Owning what I should helped to defuse the criticism. Refusing to own what was invalid helped me not to be buried by the criticism.

Paul also said that he cared only a little that he was judged by humans. In other words, what others think is important, but it isn't as important as what God thinks.

Last, Paul admitted that he didn't even judge himself. Instead, he left the situation in the Lord's hands, because he knew that in the end an omniscient God would judge him, not fallible and ignorant men. That's why he could leave his reputation in the throne room of heaven.

Even though Hannah didn't have a New Testament at hand, she, like Paul, allowed God to be her judge. Furthermore, although she could not have known Paul's injunction in Romans 12:18—"If it is possible, as far as it depends on you, live at peace with everyone"—she apparently decided that she would commit herself to the Lord's help and mercy and let Peninnah's words take their course. Perhaps Hannah knew pain has a way of growing up the child in us.

Because Hannah had chosen God as her personal focus, she was able to refocus on Him when trouble rocked the very foundations of her life. She said in effect, "God is the God of my barrenness, my pain, and if He wills, He shall be the God of my children, the God of my relationships and of my pleasure!" To live out our faith focus in whatever circumstances we find ourselves is what the Christian life is all about. To come to a point of inner praise and heart peace—to be able to say, "When I can't praise Him for what He has allowed, I am going to praise Him for who He is in what He has allowed"—is where pain comes under control.

PREPARING FOR THE BAD TIMES

Hannah must have practiced turning to God in the good times before the bad times ever came along. After all, she did such a terrific job when trouble did arrive! To practice accepting the good things God gives and developing a deep appreciation for His gifts really helps when we are in deep need. Don't expect to start praying effectively in crisis. It doesn't work that way. Try establishing a moment-by-moment, open relationship with God, where you thank Him continually for all His benefits. This helps you not to blame Him when He, the giver of all gifts, withholds one of those blessings from you.

As the Scripture says, our God is "the giver of all good gifts." A giver of gifts has every right to give or to withhold; He is under no obligation to do either. But a day-by-day experience of thanking Him for His gifts and an open communication between you and God through prayer awakens you to the reality of the benefits He daily showers upon you.

In the words of the song, "Count your many blessings, name them one by one. And it will surprise you what the Lord has done." If you practice praise, you begin to discover the generosity of your heavenly Father. This cuts short any blaming or suspicion of His dealings with us when trouble hits. There is no hint in Hannah's prayer that she was angry with God. Blame stops us from receiving help from the only One who can give it to us—namely, the Lord.

Because we may find ourselves without priest or pastor to turn to in times of trouble, it's imperative that we practice an intimate walk with God *now*. The naturalness of Hannah's conversation with God tells me her relationship with her Lord was practiced, intimate, and trusting—and *that* only comes with time. Above all, Hannah refused to blame God. Praise had helped her to do that.

SURVIVING AND REVIVING

Crises are a part of life, and Christian parents who want to pass on a vibrant faith in God to their children must learn how to handle problems of many sorts. The Scripture is replete with examples of people surviving (and what's more, reviving!) in the most difficult of trials. Take Jeremiah as one example. His enemies lowered him into a slime pit where he sank up to his neck in the stuff. He found himself up to his eyeballs in muck, but still he was able to say, "I called upon Thy name, oh Lord, out of the low dungeon. Thou hast heard my voice. Hide not Thy ear at my breathing—at my cry. Thou drawest near in the day that I called upon Thee: Thou saidst, Fear not" (Lam 3:55-57, KJV).

Judy:

Or, what about Hagar? Talk about a woman who had to overcome a lot. At different points in her life she was a slave woman, a baby machine, a nanny to her own child, a single parent, an outcast, a homeless person... and yet she was also a survivor (Gn 16-21). Twice, she found herself in the desert facing certain death.

The first time, she fled because Sarai "mistreated" her after Hagar had "despised" her mistress (Gn 16:4-6). The angel of the Lord found her by a well of water and asked her what was the matter. Hagar explained the situation and then the angel told her to return to Sarai—everything was in God's hands. Hagar returned and gave birth to a son, Ishmael.

On the second occasion, Abraham sent Hagar and Ishmael into the desert after Ishmael had mocked his brother, Isaac, during Isaac's party (Gn 21:8-14). The food and water Abraham had given them was soon gone, and Hagar put her son under a bush and left him there because she couldn't bear to watch him die. Once again, however, God intervened. "God heard the boy crying, and the angel of God called to Hagar from heaven and said to her, 'What is the matter, Hagar? Do not be afraid'" (Gn 21:17). God put the pieces back together and helped Hagar and Ishmael become their own family.

Hannah, like Jeremiah and Hagar, was to learn that she was heard by God. Yes, both Jeremiah and Hannah wanted *out* of their particular pit, but God was intent on saving them *in* it before He ever delivered them *from* it.

Jill:

Perhaps you feel like Hannah. Maybe there is another woman in your husband's life or you long for children but can't seem to conceive. Maybe you have a personal problem you cannot share with anyone. Are you emotionally drained or do you feel spiritually empty, rejected, abandoned, and disillusioned by your spiritual leaders?

If so, focus on God. Turn to Him who can meet you in the dark places, give you His comfort and counsel, and send you back into the same situation a different person.

Just as He did for Hannah.

~

Dig a Little Deeper:

These ideas can be used for further study on your own or in a group.

God intends us to count on the fellowship of believers for help and support. The problem with the church is that it is made up exclusively of sinners. No matter how bad things seem to be, try to find a group of Christians in the local church to meet with. Remember what the Lord says about the church and what He expects from it.

Discuss

1. Ephesians 4:3 tells us we must make every effort to do what?

2. In Ephesians 4:11-14 Paul lists different people God has gifted and given to the local church to help people. Make a list of these people. Then think about how their gifts could help you in your Christian parenting—especially in times of crisis.

3. If you don't already have one, consider starting a support group. Information for how to do so is on page 191.

Prayer

Pray for parents in crisis.
Pray that your local church will have viable ministries that will assist parents who are in trouble.
Pray for yourself.

F I V E

I never saw my father go fishing without first kissing my mother goodbye and saying something like, "I'll bring you a big one back." And he really did expect that his expectations would be met. It's the same with prayer. We must expect God to answer our prayers—especially for our "little, big fish." That's how fishermen think!

~

A Mother's Prayer Life

Jill:

WHEN IS THE BEST TIME TO PRAY for your children?
Hannah's example suggests it's before they're even born.
"I prayed for this child," she said of Samuel.

Stuart's mother told me once she prayed for her two
boys before they were even conceived. Once she discovered herself pregnant and assembled the nursery furniture, she and her husband would enter the nursery every
night before they went to bed. They would pray over that
empty crib with their little children in mind. It is no surprise to me that both her "little, big fish" have served
God around the world. Hannah's prayers *worked!*

They had been prayed for moment by moment, day by
day, month by month, as year followed year. Hannah
prayed for unborn children, too. Yet it seemed the heav-

ens were brass and God was occupied. One thing about Hannah, she never gave up. I would like to think she established her prayer habits when she was a child herself. As a believing Israelite woman, married to a priestly man, she would be as familiar with prayer as breathing. We don't know at what age Hannah decided to have a prayer plan all of her own, but I suspect it would have been when she was very young.

PLAN TO HAVE A PLAN

That's the first thing we all need to do—have a prayer plan of our own. If we don't have a plan, our devotions will be haphazard and perhaps ineffective. We can plan to pray, make a lifelong habit of it and join forces with God and His angels in the battle against the enemy of our families and our souls.

What do I mean by a plan? First, I mean we must plan to have a plan. Decide it will be a priority. Just as you feel it's important to plan to spend time with your husband and kids, decide it's important to plan to spend time with the One who made your husband and kids.

If you set about planning a personal prayer plan all of your own, you'll be in good shape when trouble comes or when you have to wait for your prayers to be answered. It doesn't matter how young, old, or middle-aged you are, either. Just plan to have a plan, whatever your age.

It was obvious that Hannah had a plan. The Bible says she prayed each year at a given time and place. She had not only planned to pray, she had obviously formed a habit. Even after the asked-for baby arrived, she and her husband still traveled to Shiloh every year to say their special prayers and offer their sacrifices of praise.

Habits are formed by doing something over and over again until it seems unacceptable not to do whatever it is you've decided to do. A habit is repeated behavior. It helps to repeat this behavior in the same place and at the same time. Hannah did that. She found a place and chose a time. This is very important, especially when you have decided to have a plan and form a habit—and you have children. You need to find a still point in the middle of the perpetual motion around you. You need to find a sanctuary. Jesus said, Go into your room and close the door (Mt 6:6). He obviously meant for you to go somewhere that affords you some privacy.

"Now, how do you expect me to do that?" I can hear you object. "With preschool children, it seems well-nigh impossible."

I have often told the story of my years of mothering three preschoolers. We lived in a tiny house in England. So often in the notorious English weather the little ones and I would be shut up together for days on end watching the gray skies, listening to the constant drip of the soft rain. It was good for the complexion, but bad for a mother's nerves. How was I ever to have a prayer plan, form a habit, and find a place to be apart? Our house was so very small, so very noisy, and so very full!

In the end (after praying about it), my eyes alighted on the children's playpen. It was ideal for the job, so I got in and put the kids out. Replete with English cup of tea and biscuit, Bible notebook and prayer list, I planned my plans and I formed my habit. I had found my place. I remember David, Judy and Pete rattling the bars trying to get in (the only time I can remember them wanting to get *in* rather than *out*!).

"What are you doing, Mommy?" inquired David.

"I'm meeting with Jesus," I replied sweetly, reveling in my comparative solitude.

"Judy, can you see Jesus?" inquired my persistent son of his four-year-old sister.

"No," answered my ever down-to-earth daughter. "Where is He, Mommy?"

I didn't bother explaining. The children soon began to realize it was to their advantage to leave well enough alone while Mother was in their playpen. Not too long ago David recounted my old habit in his own church pulpit. "We kids discovered that Mom was a lot nicer mom when she climbed out than when she climbed in!" (I was embarrassed!)

The practice made a mark on our two oldest children, David and Judy, who remember it quite clearly. (Wouldn't *you* remember your mother drinking tea in your playpen?) The larger lesson, of course, was not lost on them. Jesus and Mom met every day in a certain place and usually at a set time—and it was very important to leave them alone together.

Judy:

BE SPECIFIC IN YOUR PRAYERS

Another principle of Hannah's prayer life is seen in 1 Samuel 1:11. Hannah was very specific in what she asked for. She didn't say, "Please give me a child." She specifically asked for a son.

When we pray, we need to be as specific as possible in our requests. Not that God needs to know this in order to figure out what we want—God knows before we even ask what we really want. This instruction is for our own benefit. Sometimes we may not know exactly what we want, but in talking through our ideas and feelings with the Lord, we may come to a better realization about what we are feeling and why we are feeling this way. This may help us to get to the root of our problems. Also, if we are specific in our prayers, it is easier to see when and how those prayers are answered.

When I was in my second year of graduate school, I spent hours and hours working at a computer terminal. Although the computer may be the most efficient instrument to come along in a long time, it can also be one of the most frustrating. I had spent hours trying to write a program and it just wasn't working. The computer center had closed for the evening, and I was feeling very sorry for myself. I prayed, "Lord, help me." Then I tried to be more specific in my prayer. "Lord, I really need someone to help me figure out what I'm doing wrong," I said, "because otherwise, I won't be able to complete the assignment by the due date."

I secretly suspected this was a futile prayer, since everyone who knew anything had left for the evening. But no sooner had I prayed than a message appeared on my screen from a friend of mine who was a computer consultant. He had logged onto his account in a different building and noticed that I was on my account. All the message said was, "What's happening, do you need some help?" God answered a very specific prayer!

On the other hand, there may be times when we don't know what to ask for specifically. We should still bring our concerns to God. Or, maybe we're having a difficult time praying specifically for someone we love. Mom has told me that during my teenage years, she found it difficult to pray for me objectively. Her anxiety about all the things that could go wrong for a teenage girl at times almost paralyzed her prayer life.

Her solution? She asked another mother to "trade" daughters when it came to prayer. She found it a lot easier to pray for someone else's children than her own. In addition, she found it easier to think of tangible and specific things for others to pray for her daughter when she wasn't the one doing the praying.

Jill:

This idea of asking someone else to pray for my child came to me during my quiet time one morning. I was reading the story of Moses in the bulrushes. I realized the dilemma Moses' mother faced. Pharaoh's soldiers were trying to kill her son. She must have been out of her mind with worry. She put the baby in the little ark and set him among the bulrushes as a desperate last attempt to save his life.

Did she choose that spot because she knew Pharaoh's daughter usually came down to bathe at that particular place? We're not told. We do know she went home, perhaps not able to bear to watch what happened. But she left someone behind, Miriam, Moses' big sister. It was Miriam that watched breathless as Pharaoh's daughter rescued the child.

As I thought about that incident, I saw myself in Moses' mother. I was almost paranoid, expecting some crocodile or soldier to get at my baby. I was so anxious, I couldn't watch and pray. But I could find a Miriam, a sister in the Lord who would stand on the riverbank of life for me and intercede for my child. So that is exactly what I did.

God has given Stuart and me many Miriams as we have reared our children while I have been a Miriam for other friends who needed someone to care and pray for their children. Mothers, we can pray for each other and we will find peace flooding our anxious hearts.

BE PERSISTENT

Persistence is nine-tenths of the job when it comes to prayer, and Hannah is a prime example of it. We must never stop praying that our children come to know the Lord. Who will pray for children like their mother? And when we pray about it, we'll be reminded that God alone can bring about the miracle of regeneration, just as God alone can fuse an egg and sperm. God gives life!

The Lord Jesus told a story about a persistent widow whose request was honored because of her importunity. She had faith that said "thank you" for the answer that God wanted to give her, not the one she dictated—a faith that praised Him before the answer was ever given.

But persistence in waiting for God to answer prayer can cause us to change the things we ask for. I wonder if Hannah started off praying for a baby. Then when one didn't arrive, I wonder if she began to think of the reasons she wanted that child. Perhaps she thought about how she could raise the little one to serve God. Then when year followed year, maybe she concluded that the most important thing in all the world was that if a baby ever came, the child should serve God alone—even if it meant she would never rear him herself.

I don't know if that happened, but I do know in my own experience that waiting for answers gives me the opportunity to pray on about something, altering my requests until they are more in line with His will. Waiting on the Lord, and not the answer, causes us to tune in to His mind on the matter. It is often after time has tempered our requests that our prayer "works."

Wouldn't we all love to pray prayers that work! And yet it occurs to me we should praise God for the prayers we have prayed that God *hasn't* answered. Like a loving Father gently denying the cries of His children when He knows what is ultimately the best for them, so God withholds in grace the answers to some of our requests, choosing to answer them in a far better way. The secret of prevailing prayer is, after all, "not us getting God to do what *we* want Him to do, or even God getting us to do what God wants to do. Prayer is getting God to do what God wants to do."[1] Unanswered prayer can help us to lock into God's mind and will and cooperate in His mysterious purposes. Once we have learned how to do that, we will have begun to pray prayers that work. Not prayers that accomplish *our* will, but *His* will.

TRANSFORM WORRY INTO SONG

When you start to worry about the spiritual needs of your children who need the Lord, take a cue from Hannah and sing a song to your frightened heart and remind yourself God delights to give life. Sometimes we fall into the trap of believing our kids will only have a chance to be born again if we are with them twenty-four hours a day. In many years of youth work, I have concluded I must never shortchange what the Holy Spirit will do when mother is nowhere to be seen.

Over and over again in drug dives or coffee bars I have miraculously bumped into youngsters who needed the Lord. I have had the joy of introducing them to Christ, discovering in the process that I was simply the answer to a parent's prayer. Sometimes we need to trust God to bring the person of spiritual influence who can do what we cannot into our children's orbit.

I have discovered, as I'm sure Hannah did, that praise is the oil that keeps you going when you're waiting for God to move.

Have you ever wondered whatever Hannah filled her time with once she returned home, folded up Samuel's clothes, smiled at Peninnah's sour face and gave Elkanah his supper? She filled it with praise. I don't mean she did nothing but sit around singing praise choruses, but she certainly took time to compose a psalm or two (how can we know if the one we have recorded was the only one?). She was talented and she was musical and she was also clever with her hands.

I can see her busily making Samuel a little tunic to wear over his priestly garments (1 Sm 2:19), a little tunic she would take months to weave and embroider. She would carry it with her when she visited her son in Shiloh each year. And while she sewed, I'm sure she sang. Look at the words of her song and it will give you a pattern of praise.

My heart thrills to the eternal
My powers are heightened by my God
My lips exalt over my foes
for I joy in Thy deliverance.   [Moffatt's translation]

God is the giver of laughter. The psalm in chapter 2 opens with the most incredible words as Hannah is finally able to say, "My heart rejoices in the Lord" (and not my circumstances!). Hannah discovered through prayer that God will always give you something your heart can laugh about when everyone around you is in tears. She also discovered God gave life as well as laughter. "The eternal kills—the eternal life bestows," (vs. 6, Moffatt) she sang. Incredibly, she offered God this song of praise even though the previous verse tells us "and Hannah left him [Samuel] there." *There*, living with Eli and his sons, Hophni and Phinehas.

And yet she gave thanks. How easy it is after a period of intense prayer to see God graciously answer, and then to rudely forget to say thank you, or even continue meeting with the Lord once the crisis is over. Once when Jesus healed ten lepers He sent them away to show themselves to the priest to certify they were healed. They went quickly, ecstatic to see their skin and flesh full and whole again. But even before they arrived at the temple, one of the ten realized he hadn't thanked Jesus. So he turned back and fell at His feet in thanksgiving. Jesus asked, "Didn't I heal ten? Where are the nine?" They were too busy enjoying their answer to prayer.

I try very hard to make sure I make room for thanksgiving and prayer in my prayer plan. Whether I'm waiting or receiving, I meet with Him with gratitude. I don't want to be one of the nine.

FREE TO BE FREE

Finally, Hannah sings about God, not only as the giver of laughter and life but also as the giver of liberty (1 Sm 2). She had discovered through prayer and praise that the

Lord was her source of inner freedom. Even though she was trapped in a difficult marriage situation, she was free inside. "He raises the poor from the dust, and lifts the needy from the ash heap," she said (vs. 8). How poor she had felt. For a woman in her culture to be childless was poverty indeed. But He lifts up those who feel like a nothing, a nobody.

What freedom of spirit she expressed when her actions were criticized. Who would criticize her, you might wonder? Peninnah, for starters. Her family, her neighbors, and friends may have chipped in, too. Certainly her enemies would have had a heyday. It was in prayer and praise Hannah found help and relief when the stinging accusations flew in her direction. "What sort of a mother are you?" one might have said. In answer Hannah comforted herself with the words, "The Lord is a God who knows, and by him deeds are weighed" (1 Sm 2:3). Read Samuel 1:21-24 and you'll be encouraged, as Hannah was, to do the thing that you and God have agreed upon for the spiritual well-being of your child. Then leave your vindication to Him. God gives us liberty to do what is right and rejoice about it.

When Stuart and I went into full-time Christian work, several people, including a few family members, could not understand us "doing this to our children." After all, Stuart was in a solid position in banking and I was a schoolteacher. What would happen to our financial security and to the children's future? What about their schooling, travel, and sports opportunities? How irresponsible we seemed to them.

As we prayed earnestly about our decision, we found not only peace and tranquility in our hearts, but a huge sense of joy as well. We were free to be free of these material concerns. He was calling us to serve Him for higher stakes, and a more secure future for us all than we could ever provide for ourselves. We stood before Him in prayer, committed our little family into His loving care, and took a huge leap of faith into the dark. Of course, He landed us safely on higher ground. Surely He *is* the giver of laughter, life, and liberty!

Judy:

PRAYER FOR THE BIRDS WHO HAVE FLOWN

Prayers for children do not end when the kids leave home. At that time, you might have to become a little more creative about how everyone in the family can keep in touch with everyone else's prayer requests. And yet, the same principles just described will apply to your praying at this time in your life. One thing that we have discovered as a family is that since praying became such a part of our routine as children, it is still a part of our routine as adults. It's just that different methods of family prayer have worked at different times in the family life cycle.

When we began to spread around the country and each sibling began his or her own family, Mom decided that a roaming prayer letter would help everyone keep in touch with each other's concerns and victories. A large manila envelope began with one member of the family. Inside was a sheet of paper for every couple or family. The couple or family would read everyone else's entries, record their requests, and mail it to the next family on the list. This was a wonderful way to keep in touch and it worked.

Since the prayer letter was phased out, different members of our family have had to climb some steep mountains in their lives. The rest of us have supported these members through these times through prayer. It has been during these times that God has taught me a lot about my own prayer life.

First, I think I understand what it means in 1 Thessalonians 5:17 to pray continually for something. There have been times over the last few years when I can honestly say that I have been praying all day for something even as I've gone about my other duties. It is an inexplicable blessing to be in constant contact with God. You truly feel the peace described in Philippians 4. Unfortunately, I do not live every day of my life in this state, but that is something I'm striving for.

Second, I learned to be patient. I am a very systematic person and want to know the answers to question "a" before moving on to question "b." God has taught me that I may have to pray about something for a long time before I receive a definite answer. Think of how long Hannah must have prayed for a child!

Third, I learned to praise God for the little victories even though the big picture still appeared bleak. I believe that we can always find something to praise the Lord for. Most times, we are quick to criticize when our situation doesn't change soon enough to suit us but slow to praise when the answer comes.

The Lord has taught our family many lessons through praying for each other. Looking back, we can rejoice that He is all that we need Him to be, when we need Him to be—all that we need. Above all, our family is being taught the power of linking our prayers on behalf of each other. We make new prayer promises and plans each year, and we have a growing new appreciation for our family's fellowship in the gospel. We are certainly discovering anew that one of the biggest blessings of life is indeed a regenerate family!

Jill:

THE HARD PART AND THE HIDDEN PART

Hannah's prayer plan paid off. Her habit proved to be the decisive conduit of divine help and blessing. She did the hard part and God did the hidden part. She learned through the medium of prayer to depend on Him fully.

Whenever I read the story of Hannah, I am reminded of Amy Carmichael. She was a missionary who served children most of her life. She set up and ran a rescue shop for children sold or stolen for temple prostitution in India. Occasionally unscrupulous men would raid the compound and spirit a child away, most were never to be heard of or seen again. Amy would mourn as if the little one were her own, and then she would get down to prayer. Amy had a plan, a prayer plan, a lifelong habit which stood her in good stead when her children found themselves in desperate straits. Amy saw God keep most of her children safe in the midst of evil and bring some of them back to her arms. There have been many times I have borrowed her words. Perhaps you would like to do the same.

Father, hear us, we are praying,
Hear the words our hearts are saying,
We are praying for our children.

Keep them from the powers of evil.
From the secret, hidden peril,
Father, hear us for our children.

From the whirlpool that would suck them,
From the treacherous quicksand, pluck them,
Father, hear us for our children.

From the worldling's hollow gladness,
From the sting of faithless sadness,
Father, Father, keep our children.

Through life's troubled waters steer them,
Through life's bitter battles cheer them,
Father, Father, be Thou near them.

Read the language of our longing,
Read the wordless pleadings thronging,
Holy Father, for our children.

And wherever they may bide,
Lead them home at eventide.

What are your circumstances? Which of your children
is far away, in danger, in trouble, or doesn't know the
Lord? Have you made a plan? A prayer plan, making time
with God a habit? If not, why not start? Can you praise
Him as Hannah praised Him, singing, "My heart rejoices
in the Lord" (and *not* my circumstances)? If your heart is
focused on yourself or your circumstances, there is little
hope of joy. But when we focus on God and make our
requests known to Him, I have found that He is able to
make us laugh again when, humanly speaking, there is
very little to laugh about.

Isn't it time to pray?

Dig a Little Deeper:

These ideas can be used for further thought and study on your own or in a group.

Discuss

1. Read over Hannah's prayer in 1 Samuel, chapters 1 and 2. How would you contrast her prayers in chapter 1? How would you contrast her prayers in chapter 2?

Would you say that some were right and some were wrong?

Some Practical Ideas

1. Making a prayer plan.
   - Spend time with your schedule. Find ten minutes every day for God.
   - Put it down on your calendar.
   - Decide where you'll meet Him and write that on your calendar. (It might be a different place some days.)
   - Get equipped.
     a) Do you have a Bible with print big enough to read?
     b) Do you have a notebook and pencil?
   Then you are ready.
   - Make a prayer list for five days of the week. Make a new one each week.
   - Do it. And enjoy it.

2. If you have children away from home, you might want to start a family prayer letter to keep all of you in touch. Here is how ours evolved. I instigated it by sending out the original letter.

Dear Family:

Feeling a personal need to know a little more specific details of your lives so I may pray more effectively for you all, I came up with an idea that I think would bring us all closer together as a family. Just fill in your page, put everything in a stamped addressed envelope and send to the next person on the chart. If we pass this on within *one* week of receiving the package it should take *one* month to do the rounds.

With all of us being so far apart, I think we need to work hard to build our relationships over the miles and I don't know any more effective way to grow closeness than in the soil of prayer. Let's try it. When you get your letters, read them and pray for the needs during the week. (If you decide *when* to do it together, it will get done.) Each month you discard the last list and use the new one. I know we all pray for one another, but I have a feeling we are not using this hidden resource for each other like we could.

Luv, Mom

P.S. The request can be ministry related, work related, play related, life related, and hopefully personally related —anything you wouldn't ask anyone outside of family to pray about. Needless to say our family prayer letter will be *strictly confidential.*

("Are we allowed to write editorial comments on each other's requests and comments?" one of the kids inquired. "Sure! Fun!" I replied.)

I sent a list of suggestions to help it run smoothly:

   a) Let's try and turn it around within forty-eight hours.

b) Leave it on the kitchen table until done.

c) A six-month chart to remind who sent it to whom.

A few encouraging reminders followed:

Dear Family:

Well done! New reminders:

1. Pray for all requests.
2. Pull yours out and keep—put new prayer requests in.

Send on—keep it up!

Philippians 4:4

—Mom

A piece of paper for each family was put in a large envelope along with stamped addressed envelopes to the next in line. As it came to each family, they extracted the old letter and added the new one.

Prayer

Pray about your prayer plan.

Pray for your children that know the Lord.

Pray for your children who don't!

S I X

The problem with being a "real" fisherman is it can become obsessive, especially if you've had a few trips when the fish aren't biting. You know they are out there, but they are not letting on that they know you are there. Sometimes it's good to just let it out and do something else for a while. If you jump when the fish tell you to, you are in real trouble.

~

Let It Out, Let It In, Let It Go

Jill:

A BIG PART OF THE KEY TO PEACE in regard to our family has been the principle of relinquishment. We must learn to trust God with the ultimate welfare and destiny of those we love most dearly.

I learned that lesson when I was a young woman. I already had three children so, unlike Hannah, I was not praying for a child, I was praying for a husband. Specifically, I was praying that the husband I had would be around more often.

Stuart was an evangelist and that meant long separations. I prayed and prayed that God would let my husband stay home. Like Hannah, I became absorbed with my problem. I, too, had a downcast face reflecting a depressed spirit. There were many tears shed into my pillow during the long, lonely nights.

But there came a point when, like Hannah, I was able to give it up. I stopped insisting that my will be done and began accepting that His will be done. The peace that followed that acceptance of my circumstances was indescribable. Certainly my face was no longer downcast. My spirit revived and I began to get on with my life. I was even able to praise Him for the situation and trust Him for whatever answer He would see fit to give. Eight long years later He moved our family to the U.S.A. and Stuart stayed home. How thankful I am that I didn't waste that time wringing my spiritual hands and being miserable!

Hannah became a model for me throughout my ordeal. What a contrast is recorded in her prayer life. When we meet her she is frustrated and agitated. She cries as she prays. She experiences a familiar sick feeling in the pit of her stomach every time she visits the temple.

But there came a point when she gave it all into His hands. Even if God heard and answered her prayers, she promised Him she would not keep the child. "I will give him up," she promised in chapter 1, verse 11. What a relief to come to the point of relinquishment and acceptance! Truly in acceptance lies peace.

Hannah was able to get on with her life. The Bible says, "Her face was no longer downcast" (1 Sm 1:18). Did she have a baby? Not then, but she was at peace without one. God's will would be done and she was given God's assurance that she could thank Him in advance for whatever He would do. Prayer was the place that Hannah was able to accept God's provision for her in her childlessness.

DO YOU HAVE TO SEE FISH JUMP?

Of course, these lessons don't come easy! Years ago I had been crying out to the Lord in anger and frustration;

I had been doing some heavy praying and seeing no results. One day, sitting by a small lake very early one morning (I had gone there to pray), the Lord seemed to say to me, "The lake is beautiful, isn't it?"

"Yes, Lord," I answered.

"Do you believe there are fish in the lake?" He asked me next.

"Of course, Lord," I answered. "I *know* they are there."

"How do you know?" He inquired.

I looked at the glasslike surface of the water and asked myself, "Well, how *do* I know they are there?" I realized God was addressing a heart problem of mine. I wanted to know why I hadn't seen any answers to some pretty fervent prayers, why there hadn't been any visible signs of God's working. Things around me had looked just like the glass surface of that beautiful body of water I was looking at—no signs of life at all.

Then the Lord said to me, "Jill, do you have to see a fish jump to believe they are there?"

I sat still for a long time. At last I was able to say, "No, Lord, if I never see a fish jump, I will believe they are there." In other words, if I don't *see* the answer to my prayers, I *will* believe in faith that God *is* active and that there is divine action taking place below the apparently placid exterior of the situation. When that was settled, like Hannah, I was able to go on my way rejoicing and my face was no longer sad.

RESIGNATION ISN'T ACCEPTANCE

There is a definite difference between resignation and acceptance. Elisabeth Elliot, who has had good reasons to be frustrated and agitated in her life, has an excellent statement on just what that difference is.

Only in acceptance lies peace not in
resignation or in busyness.
Resignation is surrender to fate.
Acceptance is surrender to God.
Resignation lies down quietly in an empty universe.
Acceptance rises up to meet the God who
fills that universe with purpose and destiny.
Resignation says, "I can't."
Acceptance says, "God can!"
Resignation says, "It's all over for me."
Acceptance asks, "Now that I am here, what's next, Lord?"
Resignation says, "What a waste."
Acceptance asks, "In what redemptive way
will You use this mess, Lord?"[1]

Many years ago Elisabeth's husband, Jim, was killed while trying to reach a tribe of Auca Indians with the gospel. If Elisabeth had simply been resigned to fate, she would have said (as many indeed were saying), "What a waste." Instead, she was able to accept the trouble that had come to her family for whatever reason God had allowed the trouble to come.

Accepting it as the permissive will of God, she asked, "In what redemptive way will you use this mess, Lord?" Acceptance then became a springboard for action. She set off back into the jungle, along with her daughter and another widow, Marge Saint, and her daughter, to live among the tribe that had murdered their husbands. The tribe accepted them and many eventually came to Christ.

The manner in which Elisabeth and Marge handled that crisis had profound effects upon their daughters, who love and serve the Lord to this day. Those mothers were intent first and foremost on sharing their faith with their daughters, not least as they modeled acceptance, fortitude, and resilience in their common loss.

Hannah, like Elisabeth Elliot, did not simply resign herself to the inevitable. She prayed on, leaving the timing and the manner of the answer to her prayers safely in God's hands. She prayed in faith, believing that one day God would agree to give her a child. But she went a step further, promising God that if a baby did come, she would give him up, whatever the cost. She would give him up to God's will and work. She yielded her heart's desire for a child into God's arms before she ever held a child in her own!

This was far more than resignation to fate. This was faith in God's purposes and praise for His power to help her work actively with the mess she found herself in. Hannah eventually gave birth to Samuel, and later gave him up. Returning to face Peninnah, Hannah wrote such a psalm of praise that Mary, the mother of our Lord, used it as the model for her own prayer at a high point in her own mothering experience.

HOW DOES RELINQUISHMENT WORK?

So how does this act of relinquishment actually work? Three little phrases may help. First of all, "let it out." Hannah let it all out. Read chapters 1 and 2 of Samuel. There you hear the voice of pain. That's the first thing we need to do when we are praying for our children, unborn or of whatever age or condition. Let it out! Cry, holler, write a letter to God if that helps—but let it out. Let your tears do the talking when all words are gone and you feel you are literally drowning in your sorrow. Just look up to

Him and say, "I *am* a prayer; read me!" Let it out.

Second, "let it in." What are we to let in? The realization that He is the answer. Not perhaps the particular answer we've been asking Him to be, but *the* answer to whatever dilemma is ours. In His perfect time and in His perfect way, He will answer. When I believe He is "all that I need Him to be, when I need Him to be all that I need" then comes not only peace but praise. We must let it in, swap the lightness for our heaviness, the joy for our misery.

Then third, we need to let it go. And we'll need to continue to let it go moment by moment. The thing that is given must not be taken back. There may have been times Hannah was sorry she had prayed the prayer of relinquishment, but praise drove the doubts away, as praise always does.

DON'T TAKE THE COOKIES BACK

We must not be like the little girl who was playing with her friend in the woods. The children had some cookies with them, and one of the girls suggested they build a little altar and give the cookies to God. With much earnestness they accomplished this, placed their precious offerings on the top of their altar, and retired to the woods to wait until the angels came and took them away. As is the way with small children, the time dragged on when there was no immediate action, and one little girl said impatiently to her friend, "Come on, God's had our cookies long enough—let's go and eat them!"

We must not eat the cookies. Once we have prayed our

prayers (let it out); reminded ourselves He will answer our specific requests in *His* specific way, not ours; and let go of the worry of it (let it go); we must *not* take the cookies back. That's hard, but it must be done.

As I mentioned, years ago when our Christian work necessitated me being mom and dad for a period, there came a point when I could see the kids were being adversely affected. I let it out. I assure you I did. Night after lonely night I threw my spiritual tantrums. I prayed earnestly and specifically that God would give Stuart *home* ministry so he could get to know his children and his children would get to know him.

I thought I knew exactly how this could be accomplished and so I told God there was a perfectly wonderful ministry opportunity stateside that would answer all our problems. It took a long time—too long—before I gave him to the Lord and accepted that it was all right for Him to answer my desperate prayers in His way. I never doubted He would answer me, but I had been suspicious of the manner, way, timing, or answer He would choose to give.

Once I let God's peace into my heart, I affirmed my belief that God's will (not mine) was "good, pleasing, and perfect" (Rom 12:2). And then I relaxed.

After that came the biggest test—not to take back the cookies. Especially when months went by with no relief in sight. I learned many things as I waited, not least that I had no right to try and alter God's eternal timetable. So I practiced "letting go" moment by moment, reminding myself that when I was tempted to take our destiny back into my own hands, it was too late. I had irrevocably given my husband and my kids into His capable hands.

It was eight years before God gave me my heart's

desire, but never in my wildest dreams could I have imagined how He was going to work it all out. His answer involved a move. It meant immigrating to the United States, a tearing away from our roots and our homeland to live in a very different country and culture. But it was a perfect answer.

As soon as we arrived in the United States, invitations began to arrive asking *me* to travel and speak. Hesitatingly, but encouraged by my husband, I accepted the invitations that began trickling in. Suddenly Stuart and our kids were thrown together in my absence to get to know each other in ways that would never have been possible had we stayed in England.

So if you can, let it out, let it in, and let it go—and in doing this, you'll find peace.

Judy:

IF PRAYER IS IMPORTANT TO YOU, IT WILL BE TO THEM

One of the best ways to let your children go is to begin now to teach them to pray for themselves. It's easier to relinquish their future into the hands of God when you know they have the same sort of divine connection that you do. Don't get me wrong, relinquishment is never easy, but when our kids know how to pray for themselves, some of the burden we all feel is lightened.

A good way to teach our children to pray is to begin by praying consistently in front of them. Even if it doesn't feel comfortable, keep going. It soon will. Keep praying until it becomes the most natural thing in the world. Let them see that God is in the kitchen, living room, bedroom, and even in their playpen—that you and He are friends. They need to know we can talk to Him at any time and it *always* makes a difference! If it's important to you, it will be important to them. You'll see.

Greg and I have tried to form a habit with Drew and Jordan. We pray before meals and when the kids go to bed. Sometimes Drew prays, sometimes we pray, and sometimes Drew echoes our prayers. Not only will this practice help prayer to become a significant part of our children's lives, but it may be used by God as a vehicle for talking with others about Jesus.

I have a good friend whose four-year-old son prays before every meal. One day this family was visiting their larger extended family, none of whom are believers. When the food was served, everyone immediately began to eat. The little boy was perplexed because no one had prayed. So, he loudly voiced his concern to his parents. The parents explained to the rest of the family that praying before meals was an important part of their lives, and would everyone mind bowing their heads while the little boy prayed? This prayer habit opened up a lot of opportunities for discussion about what values parents were teaching their children and in whom children were learning to put their trust.

(I also once heard a story about a little boy from a Christian family who visited some unbelieving neighbors for dinner. When they began eating without giving thanks, the little boy asked, "Don't you pray before you eat?" "No," they replied. "Oh," replied the boy as he grabbed a fork, "neither does my dog.")

Samuel had an ordered prayer life once he got to the

temple. No doubt his mom knew this, and the knowledge helped ease her mind about letting her boy go. Samuel had set times for his devotions and prayers, even as an apprentice or assistant to Eli. He would listen to the old man praying and realize all over again that habit helps us go on when a crisis crashes into our lives.

Eli had plenty of trouble with his kids, but he never missed saying his prayers. There would be certain prayers laid down in God's Law that needed to be prayed at certain times and on certain days: prayers for healing or well-being, for forgiveness, and for prosperity. Sometimes a woman would ask the priests at Shiloh to pray for her infertility. Perhaps Samuel would feel sorry for such a lady and remember the story his mother had told him of her own anguish and his own birth.

IT'S NOT EASY, BUT IT'S NECESSARY

Relinquishment means laying down our greatest hopes and dreams at His feet and trusting Him to do the very, very best for us and those we love. So tell Him your deepest longings and highest hopes for your own. Those prayers that He knows will truly be for their very best interest He will work out in His own good time.

So try and adjust your watches to heavenly time zones and hang in there and wait!

I have just completed my doctorate in psychology and it has been a long haul. There were many times when I felt frustrated, angry, and upset, and yet through it all I have had one constant—the knowledge that God was in control and was working out all things. In His time and not mine, I would finish. This didn't always help my state of mind, and yet it was something that I could hold on to.

When I became particularly frustrated, I would "let it out." I spent many times crying in frustration, not understanding why this was taking so long, realizing that precious resources were being used and yet not seeing immediate results.

Over time, God showed me that He was my answer and I began to "let Him in" to take complete control of this area of my life. This was not easy for me to do because I am not a patient person. I like to see results quickly. God taught me to rely on His timing and try to become more patient. I truly believe that God worked a miracle in this area of my life. My whole attitude about when I would finish began to change.

Finally, I learned to "let it go." I'd go up to my study, turn on the computer, sit down and work, and not think about when this would be finished, but just do it. During one of my quiet times, I read a poem in *Streams in the Desert* that became my special verse. I kept a copy of this verse right above my computer. Whenever I sensed myself becoming overwhelmed with the situation, I would read this poem and then "let it go" to God all over again.

> Stay firm, He has not failed thee
> In all the past,
> And will He go and leave thee
> To sink at last?
> Nay, He said He will hide thee
> Beneath His wing;
> And sweetly there in safety
> Thou mayest sing.[2]

Jill:

I don't know where you are in the child-rearing process, but perhaps you have had a recent Hannah experience. Have you left him there or left her there? Maybe you've taken your college-age kid far away across state lines and left them there. How do you feel about that?

I well remember taking Judy to college and leaving her there. It was only a three-hour drive away in the next state, but I watched her body language tell me what was going on inside her... and my own stomach began to churn. I will never forget settling her in and then taking her out for a farewell meal. The tears running down her cheeks when the salads were served were matched by mine. My poor husband looked helplessly at his wet women and wondered what to talk about. By the time the dessert was served, we were both a mess. In the end we left Judy outside her dorm and drove home in silence.

How could Hannah have written a psalm after leaving her little boy behind? There is only one answer. Only one person can give us a laughing heart at times like these— God!

When Hannah left Samuel in the place she honestly believed was the best on earth for him, her little boy didn't know the Lord. Oh, he already knew a lot about the Lord, but he didn't know him for himself. *Will he come to faith?* Hannah must have worried. She knew everyone has free will, a choice.

As she thought about this, she must have concentrated on the omnipotence of God. God is the author of life and death, she decided. Not only could He give physical life (and Samuel was living proof of that), He could give spiritual life as well. She would pray about it and then leave it in God's hands. She would relinquish her son into the loving arms of God almighty.

RELINQUISHMENT IS NOT ABANDONMENT

Never confuse relinquishment with abandonment. We must let our loved ones go—but we should never stop praying for those we love. There never comes a time when our responsibility to pray for our own is done. We can't retire.

Do you think Hannah ever quit praying for Samuel? We don't know for sure but I doubt it. As Samuel became prominent as a leader in Israel, I'm sure she felt all the more need to spend time praying for him. As a grandmother, I have found the same to be true. Not only have my prayers for our children and their families grown deeper and (I hope) more effective, I have found even more reason to pray for them than I did in their growing years.

It's really never over. Look at Eli. Eli had been a good high priest of the Lord. Things had gone well until... when? We're not sure just how it was that the old man lost control of his sons. They were even in the ministry with him. But something had gone sadly awry in that leader's family. Perhaps Eli had no Hannah to pray for him. Or maybe Eli's wife had given up on her part of the prayer battle. We don't know, but one thing is certain: the more godly and effective your children are, the more the devil will attack them.

Prayer can make the difference. A believing, prevailing

battle cry in the name of the Lord can give your children power over the devil. I have seen evidence of this in our own family. I have watched the three young couples who belong to us and who are all in varied ministries come under extraordinary stress, and I have been aware of forces trying to tear apart their lives, relationships, and ministries.

Alerted by each other, the family closes ranks at such times and begins to pray. No, the battle is never over! And I believe the battle is joined when our adult children are walking closely with the Lord and are being used of Him. There is no doubt in my mind that God intervenes and turns these situations around in answer to believing, fervent, effective prayer.

Moms, it's never over. It's true we must relinquish our children into the loving arms of God, but Hannah prayers still need to be prayed for our Samuels, however old they are.

So let it out. Let it in. Let it go. And keep on as long as you have breath.

~

Dig a Little Deeper:

These ideas can be used for further thought and study on your own or in a group.

Discuss

1. Let It Out
   Read Psalm 42. Many people believe this psalm was written by David at a low point in his life. It is full of laments and complaints. He sounds very depressed. Make a list of the reasons his soul is so disturbed. Can you relate?

2. Let It In
   David lets hope into his heart. What is hope, and according to this psalm—what difference does it make?

3. Let It Go
   David lets his dream go. He wants to be back in Jerusalem but it looks unlikely. He lays that particular dream down, and says, "I will yet praise Him."

4. Which part of the psalm has meant the most to you? Why?

A Practical Exercise

This is a prayer exercise which may help you. You may wish to share it with someone you know.

Recognize what the thing is that you need to let go.
Express your feelings about it to the Lord.
Let God come near.

Imagine yourself giving Him your pain, anger, frustration.

"Nestle" into the will of God for your life.

Quit asking for the same thing and start thanking Him for whatever answer He has for you.

Undo your spiritual grasp around your request. Let Him take it from you.

Inscribe what you have said to God in your prayer diary or Bible.

Share an appropriate part of this experience with someone.

Have fun—be happy!

Prayer

Spend a few moments telling God how you feel and the reasons.

Spend a few moments "letting go" some promises of God. Just repeat Scripture verses you know.

Spend a few moments relinquishing control. Give it to God.

Spend a few moments praying for those you know who need to do the same.

SEVEN

Do you know how many books there are about fishing? Hundreds! You can't become really good at the art without reading at least one or two of them. They tell you all about the varieties of fish, where they are, what bait to use, when the fish are biting, and how to land them. That last thing is very important. I never heard my father say, "I influenced an awful lot of fish today!" He either caught them or he lost them. We need to remember that.

Keep Them near the Ark

Judy:

HANNAH WANTED THE BEST for her son. She wanted him to live under the sound Word of God, just as we should want our children to be under the sound word of God. The Bible tells us in 1 Samuel 3:3 that Samuel slept near the ark of the covenant. The ark was the receptacle for the Ten Commandments and represented the presence of God. In other words, Samuel slept in God's presence. God was always with Him, and Samuel was very aware of this reality.

Although our children cannot sleep next to the ark of the covenant, we can try to get them as near as possible to the Word of God. We can teach them the Ten Commandments and be aware that God is always with them and they are always in His presence. They can't know all of this if we don't tell them.

Because our society has become so compartmentalized, many people expect the church to teach their children everything about God. We must be teachers at home. We are so fortunate to have a multitude of resources to help us with this task. I am amazed at the number of scripturally based songs and videos that are available. Whenever we are riding in the car, Drew asks for Christian tapes. He knows most of the words to each tape. The exciting thing about this is that the tapes are Scripture verses set to music. Basically, Drew is memorizing Scripture. These tapes are so much a part of our car routine that when I am on my way to work without the children, I've found that it takes me about fifteen minutes to realize that I am playing their music. Although I love their tapes, it is nice to listen to my own music sometimes.

Jill:

It was always a priority for us as parents to try and craft a stimulating and helpful personal reading plan for each child. Make sure each little one has a readable Bible at their own reading level. It's a bit like a pair of shoes—they grow out of the old pair into new ones that fit better. Stuart and I opted for a method of Bible reading rather than just a Bible story book, but both can be used in a reading plan. (See the section at the close of this chapter.) We all learn far more when we figure it out for ourselves than taking something secondhand.

We lent a hand, sitting in while the kids did their reading, asking them about it or being there to pray together when they had finished. As children develop, it is important to talk over the material and method you've chosen, remembering that children change. That may mean a change in their devotional helps, as well.

Judy:

When I was a teenager, I had a tough time finding a devotional book that really interested me. Mom decided to help me out. Each day when I returned from school, I would find a different devotional book on my bed. The next morning when I went downstairs for breakfast, Mom would ask me how I'd liked it. I was going through a stage in my life when I wanted to choose for myself and I didn't take kindly to a lot of questions. One day I had had enough of what I considered nagging. So I turned to Mom and said, "If you bug me one more time about my devotions, I promise you, I will never read the Bible again!" She replied, "All right," and slowly walked to her room.

Years later, Mom told me that after our encounter she rather dramatically flung herself on her knees, decided that she had cut my spiritual ear off, and worried that I would go on drugs and die. In her mind she held my funeral and witnessed to a lot of people. At that point she turned in her Bible to the story of Jesus' companion in the Garden of Gethsemane who cut off the ear of the high priest's servant (Lk 22:47-53). She said, "See, God, just like in this story—I cut off Judy's ear!" Patiently, God told Mom to be quiet and read on in the story. It was as if God were saying to her, "You may have cut her ear off, but just as I put the servant's ear back on, I can do the same for Judy—if you will just be quiet and let me work."

Mom realized that she could provide all of the resources and opportunities for me, but in the end, I had to find Jesus my own way. Instead, she expected me to accept Him the same way she had. This is a hard lesson for Christian parents because we so badly want our children to know Him and love Him. And yet sometimes we can actually destroy the very thing we are trying to nurture if we push too hard.

FIND A BIBLE-TEACHING CHURCH

What exactly do we mean by rearing our kids under the sound Word of God? Part of this involves finding a church that teaches the Bible. This may take some shopping around. One of the blessings of living in America is the freedom we have to worship God, but with that freedom comes many variations of Christianity. Make sure that the church you attend teaches the Word of God.

Since I left home for college, I have had the pleasure (and sometimes, displeasure) of finding new church homes. This has been an educational experience for me, since I grew up with sound evangelical teaching. I have been amazed by what some churches try to pass off as sound teaching from the Word of God. Some ministers didn't even refer to the Bible, while others quoted and described it inaccurately. My heart aches for children who grow up in these churches believing that they know Jesus Christ, yet in reality they have no idea who He is.

Greg and I have enjoyed teaching the New Members' class at our church. One of the most interesting classes is the one where each of the new members tells how he or she ended up at our church. Although the stories vary, there is a common thread. Somewhere in these people's pasts, they learned something about the Word of God.

Some learned and have continued to learn about God. Others were dropped off at the church door as children and learned from Sunday School. As soon as these children became old enough to make their own decisions, they quit attending church. Interestingly, however, many who left the church are now returning because they want to expose their own children to some Christian and moral teaching. It is just as important to parents today as it was in Hannah's day that children are reared under the sound Word of God.

However, not only must the sermon be scripturally based, but all of the other ministries need to be grounded in the Word of God. It has been very important to Greg and me to make sure that we are involved in a church that has a good children's education program. Our preschoolers are too young to understand a sermon; they need to have the Bible brought down to their level. We want to make sure that they can learn about Jesus even at their young age.

My sister-in-law, Libby, emphasized the importance of this idea:

When I was eight months old, Christ changed the lives of my parents who until that point were heading for a divorce. My parents immediately began to take God very seriously and His will became the driving force in their lives.

We joined a Bible teaching church where I was taught the basic tenets of the gospel almost as early as the nursery. I'm not sure if it was the formal teaching or just the nursery workers' enthusiasm about their faith that caught my attention. I began to understand that there was a really scary place called hell where

Satan lives, and I sure didn't want to live there with him. My fear of going to hell, along with the conviction of the Holy Spirit, led me to learn more about the gospel.

In my own little two-and-a-half-year-old mind, I began to believe in Jesus' love and sacrifice for me, and His desire to save me from Satan's hell and spend eternity with me. Although my understanding of theology was extremely limited, it certainly was enough for salvation. As early as kindergarten, I recall being confident that God knew me as His child.

Like Samuel, our children have to hear God's words for themselves. They have to follow Christ their own way. One of the ways my parents made this easier for me was to give me opportunities to hear His voice. They arranged for me to attend Christian camps, hear youth-oriented speakers, and go to Christian concerts. Although I may not have realized at that time that these events enabled me to get to know God, in looking back I see that many of them had a profound impact on my life.

Hannah provided the best opportunity open to her for Samuel to hear God's Word, and we must follow her example. The balance is always to do this, while yet allowing our children to find God in their own way. This may be particularly difficult when the children reach adolescence.

MINISTERING TO TEENAGERS

One of my favorite classes to teach at Trinity Evangelical Divinity School concerns adolescent development. This is fun for a number of reasons. First, everyone in the class has been through this exciting and yet at times frustrating developmental stage, and so everyone can relate with their own examples and stories. Second, this is such a crucial age for children. This is a time in their lives when they are trying to find their own identity. They are asking themselves questions such as "Who am I, where am I going, and who am I to be?"

Males and females search for their identity in different ways. Boys develop their identity through separateness and individuality. During their teenage years, they begin to prepare for their occupation, since their identity is wrapped up in their career and occupation. On the other hand, girls develop their identity through connection and relationships. Although this is beginning to change, many believe it is still generally true.[1]

Furthermore, this is a time in children's lives when peers become very important. Parents don't become totally unimportant, of course; in fact, the influence of peers varies from person to person and situation to situation. Still, adolescents spend a lot of their waking hours with their friends and greatly influence each other through praise, peer group admiration, imitation, and other forms of social reinforcement.[2]

Knowing all of these things brings me to the third and most important reason why I like teaching the class at Trinity. I believe that the church and Christians have a wonderful opportunity to minister to teenagers. Adolescents are ripe for the gospel and the church can have a profound impact in these kids' lives. Youth pastors can be great role models for adolescents by modeling Christian values, behaviors, and attitudes. In addition, influential Christian people can be there to reinforce adolescents for the positive things that they do.

I'm sure most youth pastors sometimes feel discouraged and think that they aren't having any effect at all. It would be encouraging for these people to be able to talk to the teens years later and learn what kind of impression they made. Some may be surprised at the types of things they modeled.

I was lucky to have a youth pastor who modeled Christian values. He showed me that although being a man of God and following Christ was the most important thing in his life, it wasn't a dull or boring task for him. It was exciting! He knew how to mix being serious and having fun. This was important for me at that stage of my life. I was not interested in a Christianity that was always serious and what I considered no fun.

My brother was tremendously influenced by his youth pastor:

They say we repress that which is not pleasant, which is why we can't remember our teenage years. Although that is supposed to be a joke, we realize it contains a stroke of truth. I can remember the peer pressure, the parties, the basketball tryouts and the new fascination with girls, but only in a sporadic way. One thing, however, sticks firmly in my memory. My relationship with our youth pastor, Mike, helped formulate who I would be.

What was it that made him such an effective minister? He was so gentle, so kind, so humble and unassuming. He drew no attention to himself but reflected everything to Jesus. I remember finding myself in compromising situations and asking myself, "What would Mike do in this situation?" Because Mike so thoroughly lived his life for Jesus, I soon found myself saying, "I want to be like Mike!" We should never underestimate the impact a role model can have!

Since peers are so important in this stage of development, the church can provide a place for Christian peers to come together, worship Christ, and have fun. When I was a teenager, we had a phenomenal youth group—a youth pastor who was our friend but also our spiritual leader and peers who loved the Lord and enjoyed having a good time. I was very fortunate in that a lot of the youth group attended my high school; therefore, I had a Christian support group in a secular school. It was a lot easier to say no to the negative influences in my life because I had Christian friends who agreed with and supported me. There was an alternative to most of the activities that occurred.

For example, our youth group rented out the local YMCA and had an all-night lock-in for all of the teens who did not want to attend the school parties. We played games, swam, ate, had fun, and spent time learning about God. These lock-ins became so popular that they ended up being one of the most influential evangelistic outreaches provided by our youth program.

Jill:

Have you noticed the idea of "fun" keeps popping up in this chapter? My husband's philosophy on rearing children who love the Lord can be summed up in three phrases: Be fair, be firm, and be fun! He always made sure our home rang with laughter, which is a great environment in which to grow Christian commitment.

I am the spiritually intense partner in our marriage and

I find it hard to have fun. In fact, I almost have to put it on my calendar for the week: "Have fun Thursday!" But I have learned that creating an environment, not for frivolity but for healthy Christian fun, has been a huge advantage in tempering the negatives we have to lay on the children sometimes.

Involvement in church ministries can be fun and provide that necessary element. A group of peers can provide that vehicle, too. It's hard for Christian teens to keep excited with their faith if they are on their own or if their group is excited about other things. But when we provide them with a godly environment shaped by the Word of God, populated with Christian peers, and infused with fun, we vastly increase the chances of turning out young men and women who love the Lord with all their hearts.

And that's what we're after, isn't it?

~

Dig a Little Deeper:

These ideas can be used for future thought and study on your own or in a group.

Discuss

1. What do young people need in a church program?
   Which one of those elements could you provide through your local church or in your home?
2. We will not insist our children stay "near the ark" if we are not convinced ourselves of the importance of the Bible. Read 2 Timothy 2:15.
   Who are we to try to please?
   What will this entail?
   What do you think "correctly" means?
   Read Ephesians 6:4. (*Fathers* can be read as *parents.*)
   What do you think it means to not exasperate your children?
   What do you think the "training and instruction of the Lord" means?
3. Look up these verses and discuss them: Colossians 3:16 and Hebrews 4:12.
4. Read and discuss what one mother did to help her child be more involved in Sunday worship:

   If you have ever sat in the proximity of an elementary-age child in a typical Sunday morning worship service, you might see a real problem: fidgeting, whispering, poking, playing with the hymnal and visitor cards, crawling on the floor, drawing aimlessly on scraps of paper provided by mom, begging for gum, running to the bathroom or fountain... you get the point.

   Before you say, "Yes, aren't those kids just terrible! And their parents...," you need to realize the real problem. It is not the child, but rather, trying to fit him or her into our adult mode of worship. Children do not learn or listen well by lecture. Children cannot understand words and phrases prepared carefully in a weekly sermon for adults. Children learn best by doing and figuring out, by puzzles, and games, and language geared to their age level of understanding. While the message given in the worship service is for all people—young and old—the responsibility we have is to somehow take those adult thoughts and transform them so they can be easily understood by children.

That is why five years ago I started writing "Just For Kids"—a weekly children's activity bulletin based on the pastor's sermon outline and Scripture, designed to be completed during the Sunday morning worship service. In a typical "Just For Kids," I create dot-to-dot, word-finds, mazes, sentence jumbles, secret codes, funny sentence choices, arrow puzzles, crossword puzzles, and lots more—all based on biblical truths and Scripture included in the pastor's sermon. While the children are working on their activity bulletins, they will often recognize a specific puzzle they've completed is just what the pastor is talking about! Their reaction is often, "Hey, I can understand my pastor's words. He is talking to me, too!"

Preparation for "Just For Kids" makes it necessary for me to get my hands on the pastor's sermon outline by at least the Thursday before the Sunday sermon. Design and content of "Just For Kids" takes three to four hours. The original drawing of figures, dot-to-dots, mazes, etc., requires the most time, and I often wish for art classes I never had.

After the content of "Just For Kids" is finished, our church secretary skillfully arranges my material in bulletin form. What did we ever do without copier machines?

"Just For Kids" is distributed in Sunday School classes before the worship service, and at the door as kids arrive for worship with their parents. I have two elementary-age children be the "Just For Kids Hander-Outers." After all, "Just For Kids" is just for kids!

Last summer every child in our church was given the opportunity to draw a picture for the cover of "Just For Kids." A different drawing was used each week, complete with the signature of the artist! At the end of the summer, I decided to use one of our sixth-grade boy's drawings for the permanent winter "Just For Kids" cover. The kids that took part in this opportunity actually became a creating part of their bulletin.

The benefits of "Just For Kids" belong not only to the children of our church but I must claim them as well. This weekly discipline demands that I spend time studying God's Word with greater depth and with more thought than just a casual glance or pleasant peruse. Painstakingly reducing Scripture verses into words or pictures simple enough for a small child, yet exciting enough to captivate this child's busy thoughts, enables me to take a second look, a fresh look, an uncomplicated look at the promises of God I have heard and read about many times. Once again I experience "faith as a child"—and it is wonderful!

Having three children of my own—Andy, 13, Emily, 9, and David, 6—had made me aware of what children do and do not understand. The concepts presented and the wording used in my "Just For Kids" has come from my experience as a mother communicating to my children. I want them to know that Sunday worship is for them as well as for Mom and Dad, and that their Pastor Daddy is talking to them and not just the adults. I want that hour to increase their knowledge of the Savior's love, and not just be something for them to endure. The answer for our family, and for our church in Cook, Minnesota, is "Just For Kids."

—By Kathy Lutz

Resources

1. Scripture Union puts out excellent Bible reading notes for all ages. For example:

QUEST

Seven- to eleven-year-olds will discover that Bible reading is fun with the Quest Gang. Each day, Quest helps you understand a small part of the Bible.

And there are:
- codes to be solved
- puzzles to do
- things to think about
- things to pray about
- a club to join

(For more information write to: Scripture Union Bible Ministries, 7000 Ludlow Street, Upper Darby, PA 19082.)

Prayer

Pray for godly pastors.

Pray for churches who need the Word of God to be taught correctly.

Pray for Sunday School teachers who teach our children.

Pray for your own discipline and study of the Word of God.

Pray for children who are rebelling against the Word of God.

E I G H T

There's nothing quite like landing a fish. And it doesn't need to be a big one either. In my experience the little ones can be more lively than the big ones and give you a real run for your money. It's great fun to share your stories with other fishermen, too. "Real" fishermen always rejoice with a brother or sister fisherman if he's had a good catch.

Leading Your Child
to Christ

Jill:

GOD USES AN ENDLESS VARIETY OF METHODS to bring our children to a personal faith in Christ, but the key thing is *they must come*. They must take the plunge for themselves. They must decide on their own to commit their lives to God. With their own ears they must hear His call and with their own mouths they must respond. No one else can do it for them. As the saying goes, "God has no grandchildren."

Our friends David and Wendy Skroch know this well. When their son Steven was three years old they moved the family from its suburban home to Chicago, where Dave and Wendy started missionary training and language school. Four months later they moved again, this time to a provincial town in the Philippines where they continued language school and discovered the meaning of culture shock. Big rats, no water, no electricity, and no English will do that. They had heard that three-year-olds were old enough to weather culture shock, but they never dreamed that for Steven it would result in sleeplessness, night-long screaming fits, weight loss, and melancholy. After many months, the family moved to Manila, where the Skrochs began their church planting ministry in a squatter area. It was an extreme situation which could have fostered cynicism and bitterness.

Steven spent a lot of time in the slums watching his Daddy minister. Every night when Dave and Wendy tucked him in bed, they prayed with their son. One night Wendy shared God's plan of salvation very simply, using a few sentences. She didn't ask him to receive Christ but he told her that was what he wanted. And a new resident of heaven was added to the Lamb's book of life.

The Skrochs don't think it was their missionary work that gave Steven the desire to know the Lord, and they're not sure what part his personal struggles played in helping him to decide. But they believe their faithfulness to God through many trials and their prayers for Steven since before he was born are what prompted him to take notice of the Lord's call.

Steven's young faith didn't make life any easier for him; there were severe trials ahead, most notably a military coup in Manila that, in part, took place in the Skroch's own backyard! Another time Dave was stricken with a serious illness that lasted nine full months. When Steven turned ten, his mother asked him what made him desire to know the Lord. He shrugged and said, "He just called me."

A VOICE IN THE NIGHT

God spoke to Old Testament saints in a variety of ways. He talked audibly to Moses and Joshua, but His word became rare during the three centuries of rule by the Judges. By Eli's time there were no prophets speaking God's word to Israel at all, mainly because the old priest's sons were wicked.

One night when Eli was asleep and Samuel and the other priests were settling down for the night, an incredible thing happened. As the lad was about to fall asleep, "the Lord called Samuel by name. 'Samuel, Samuel,' He said." The little boy thought Eli had called for him, so he hurried to the old man and said, "Here am I." The aged priest told him he hadn't called for him and so Samuel went back to bed (1 Sm 3:4-10).

The Lord's voice sounded unfamiliar to Samuel and twice he ran into Eli's room thinking the old man had called him. In the end, Eli figured it out. "If He calls you again," he instructed, "say, 'Speak, Lord, for your servant is listening'" (vs. 9). When Samuel heard God's voice again, he did as Eli had told him.

The application of this story is simple yet vitally important. We need to be aware that God may well "speak" directly to our children. We need to be ready to help them respond, as Eli did with Samuel.

Judy:

Don't forget that at this point in the sacred story, twelve-year-old Samuel did not yet know the Lord and didn't recognize God's voice (1 Sm 3:7). Samuel had participated in and assisted with religious rituals, heard the read-

reading of the Word, and listened to people telling of what God had done for them or those they loved. He had grown in stature, in favor with God and man (1 Sm 2:26). This was a boy who had learned a lot about God—and still he did not know the Lord.

Samuel represents thousands of children reared in Christian homes who know about the Lord but don't know Him personally for themselves. Just because our children are thoroughly involved in religious activities and can cite Scripture verses and texts does not mean that they actually know God, that they have accepted Him as their personal Savior. Like Samuel thousands of years ago, there needs to come a time when our children "hear" with their inner ear the voice of God calling them into a personal relationship with Himself that results in a lifetime of service.

Jill:

KNOWING GOD PERSONALLY

Hannah did everything possible to get young Samuel into an environment where he could know God personally—really know Him. It intrigues me that Samuel was twelve years of age at the time he heard God's voice. What a prime time for faith to be led on into reality. At this age the heart is tender, the mind is open and the will is ready for adventure. But that will must be challenged to put God at the center of its plans and desires.

Never presume that just because your kids are born in a Christian home, they will automatically come to know the Lord. Don't be lulled into complacency. As Dr. Billy Graham says, "If you were born in a garage, it doesn't make you a car."

Encourage your young Samuels that they need to be

listening for the voice of God for themselves. They need to know that God doesn't speak solely to grown-ups. He can speak to them as well—even if they're junior high age, as was Samuel!

As Christian parents, Stuart and I told our children from their earliest days that God wanted to talk to them, just as much as He wanted to talk to their mommy and daddy. We also told them that because He wanted to make sure we heard what He was saying to us, He had written it all down for us in the Bible.

I remember explaining to our four-year-olds as simply as I knew how that Jesus wanted them to know four things. First, Jesus loved them so much He wanted them to live with Him forever. Second, He wanted them to know they had hurt Him by breaking some of His rules. Third, He made it clear that anyone who breaks God's rules can't go to heaven to live with Him, even though He wants them to. Last, we explained how Jesus came to earth to tell every boy or girl who was really sorry they had broken His rules that He would forgive them if they asked Him to. And those He forgave would be invited to live with Him in heaven forever.

At this point I asked our children, "Do you want to tell Jesus you're really, really sorry?" When they said, "Yes," I replied, "Would you like me to help you to say you're sorry, or do you want to tell Him yourself?" If they told me they wanted me to help (which they did), I prayed a very simple prayer and suggested they repeat it after me, sentence by sentence.

"Lord Jesus," we prayed, "I'm glad You love me and want me to come and live with You forever. Please come into my heart. I'm really sorry for breaking Your rules. Thank You for dying for me. Amen."

Judy:

SPEAKING AT THEIR LEVEL

Effective communication has a lot to do with choosing the right terms. One sure way to miscommunicate is to speak in terms inappropriate to your intended audience. Mom can speak firsthand to this truth.

We were living in England at the time and Mom had three preschoolers. One day she was asked if she would drive a missionary to the train station. Mom was thrilled for some adult company. She thoroughly enjoyed the drive, but when she stopped at the station, the missionary leaned over and said, "Can I give you a little advice? If I were you, I would try to find some adult's company with whom you can communicate." Mom looked puzzled and the missionary continued, "The whole way here you told me to look at the 'moo-cows and horseys.'"

For the opposite reason, we need to choose appropriate terms when speaking to our children about the Lord. Too often we use language that is beyond their level of comprehension.

One Friday when my brother, David, was about six years of age, Dad told him he would be going for an x-ray on the following Monday. The weekend passed and it was time to go to the hospital. "Hurry up, Dave," shouted Dad up the stairs. As they set off, my father cast a glance at my brother who was sitting bolt upright in the car, his eyes wide. "You're not scared, are you?" he asked. "Of course I'm scared!" answered Dave. "I know what an execution is!"

The amazing thing was he showed up! That little incident reminded my parents of the need to define unfamiliar terms for their children.

I've also learned this lesson with Drew. I recently took him for his yearly checkup. After the doctor finished, I told Drew that the nurse would need to draw blood for a lead-level test. He immediately started crying. I tried to console him without much success. In between sobs, he asked, "How are they going to put it back on?" I didn't know what he was talking about so I asked him what "it" was. He said, "My arm." He thought the only way they could get blood was to cut off his arm!

I quickly assured him that all the nurse needed to do was make a small hole in his skin. Then he asked, "How will they put the cover back?" Again, I didn't know what he meant by "cover." He pointed to his skin and asked again—how was it going to be put back over the hole? I quickly realized I had not done a very good job of explaining what was about to take place.

Our difficulties only get worse when we begin discussing spiritual issues. We need to talk and relate to our children on a level they can comprehend. Jean Piaget, a famous Swiss researcher, has developed a well-known theory of cognitive development. Although this theory makes sense developmentally, we believe we must also allow for the work of the Holy Spirit in a child's understanding.

STAGES OF A CHILD'S UNDERSTANDING

Infants learn about their world through perception, sensation, and action. This is the stage when everything within arm's reach is placed in the mouth. Jordan is at this stage so whenever I enter a house, I have to quickly check to make sure all of the pieces of all of the toys are big enough so that he won't choke on them.

From the approximate age of two to seven, a child

relies heavily on actual appearance rather than reasoning. Observation is very important to children at this stage, but they can't yet understand why something is happening. These kids live in the here and now and have a limited understanding of time and space.

A famous example of children at this stage comes from Piaget's work. Children see two similar containers with equal amounts of water. A person then pours the water from one of the containers into a different shaped container, long and thin, for example. The children are then asked if the long and thin container has the same amount of water as the other container. According to these kids, the tall and thin tube has more water because the water comes to a higher level.

Since these children depend on perception to learn, we need to make sure that our teaching of the Bible and spiritual concepts is very concrete. For children at this age, play is work; therefore, we can use their play time to teach them things. If the kids are playing with blocks, we can help them build a church and explain that the church is God's house. If we're at the park with our children and they see a rabbit, ant, or butterfly, we can use the opportunity to teach them that God made all of these creatures.[1]

In addition, books with lots of illustrations also are very helpful. When we apply a Bible story to the children's lives, we need to ask appropriate questions.

Mom recently came and watched the boys for a few days while Greg and I enjoyed some rest and relaxation on our own. Mom had run after the children all day long and finally Jordan had gone down for a nap. Drew was playing happily in the playroom and Mom took the opportunity to steal a few quiet, restful moments. All of a sudden, she became very conscious of just how quiet the house seemed. Quiet, in a house where a preschooler is awake, can mean only one thing—trouble! She dragged herself out of the chair and began to scour the house for Drew. Finally, she found him by the back door. He was surprised to see her and turned to say, "Nanna, you's everywhere!" Drew cannot yet understand the concept of the omnipresence of God, yet he can understand an adult seeming to be everywhere and watching his every move.

By the time children reach the age of about seven or eight, they begin to use elementary logic. Their logic is tied to real, concrete objects and events. In other words, they do not understand symbolism. Therefore, if we are trying to use objects to teach our children at this stage, it's important that the objects are what they are and are not trying to represent something else. For example, in a child's mind "a candle is a candle; it is not [the child's] life shining to influence others for Christ."[2] If you want to use objects then try using things such as "a dainty fan sent home by a missionary... a model of Christ's tomb, or a miniature scroll with a few Hebrew words on it to show [her] the Scriptures that the children in Bible times read." Children of this age love to use art (finger painting, making posters or banners), drama, books, Bible games, and music as ways to learn.

Finally, around the age of approximately eleven or twelve, many children begin to think in abstract terms (some adults never reach this stage and are comfortable staying at the previous level). At this stage a child can be taught concepts and theological ideas. For example, you could begin to teach a child at this stage about the

Jill:

CATCHING THE MOMENT

Like Eli, we as guardians need to sense when the Lord might be calling our children to Himself. We need to be thoroughly in tune. Fortunately, Eli eventually understood what had happened to Samuel and helped him respond appropriately.

Sometimes, like Samuel, our children may run into our room to recount a dream or ask us a question. We need to take time to answer them carefully right then. This could be the time God's Spirit is calling our children by name.

If we sense this is happening, we should leave whatever we are doing (nothing is more important than our children's eternal well-being) and explain what they need to do.

Our daughter-in-law's mother was in the right place at the right time when the right questions were asked. According to Debbie:

My father was a Baptist preacher, so it seemed as if I was born in the church itself. We would never miss Sunday School, the worship service, the Sunday evening service, or midweek Bible Club. My mother was, and is to this day, a woman who loves the Lord with all her heart. She would never miss a church service—and that meant that all five of us kids, whether we felt like it or not, were going to church. Actually, we learned never to even think of not going.

I can remember going to Sunday School and learning about the blackness within my heart. I didn't like the color black. It reminded me of scary things—the dark, shadows in my room, icky thoughts. I didn't want anything to do with black, let alone have it a part of my heart.

One night, I told my mom that I wanted my heart never to be black. Black meant dirty. She then knelt with me by my bedside, and I asked Jesus to wash the blackness away and to come into my life. My mom tells me I was about five years old at the time. I have loved the Lord ever since I was young—I have always had a desire to please Him, honor Him, to have Him be Lord of my life.

Stuart's mother had a similar sensitivity to the Spirit's leading. One Sunday Stuart's brother, Bernard, was sick, so their mother kept the boys at home instead of going to church. Stuart was around the age of seven at the time and was sitting by the fire, thinking. Suddenly he jumped off the hearth seat, ran to the foot of the stairs and shouted up to his mother, "Mother, are you and Dad Christians?" "Yes," answered his mother. She instantly left her work and ran downstairs to catch the moment. She ended up leading her little boy to Christ.

I often wonder if Mother Briscoe had been out of touch that day, where we would be. And when I hear people from all over the world telling my husband they found Christ through his ministry, I wonder where they would be. And I wonder most of all what Mother Briscoe was busy doing upstairs on that oh so important Sunday, so long ago? It's so easy to get absorbed in our house-work and miss the moment. I thank the Lord for a mother who was in touch. People always need to be more mother who was in touch. People always need to be more important than our schedules. Especially our little people. Mother Briscoe believed that God's Spirit may well speak to her "little, big fish" and at any time was available when it happened.

As a mother, I came to realize bedtime was very important to my three teenagers. It's no good expecting adolescents to talk to us when we want them to—at a convenient lull in our activities, for example. Judy is a night person; she regularly wakes up shortly after 10:00 P.M. each night. It was a struggle not to flop into bed early (I'm a morning person), but I realized it was vital to hang around and catch the moment! It was in that ordinary period of time that we talked about the extra-ordinary things! Meals can be another time to catch the moment.

Judy:

My older brother Dave was five when on Easter Sunday he listened to stories in Sunday School about Jesus' death and resurrection. When the family was sitting down to eat, he started asking Mom and Dad a lot of questions, including why Jesus had to die on the cross. Dad was able to tell Dave and ask him if he wanted to ask Jesus into his life. Now Dave is a dad himself and has experienced the same thing happening with two of his own children.

Dave had the privilege of leading both Daniel and Michael to Christ during bedtime talks. Dave took time, sensing that his little, big fish wanted information that had more to do with spiritual need than putting off the bedtime hour. "It's such a relief," he said, "to know that my seven and five-year-old children know the Lord Jesus, for many never come to know Him. I'm told that 85 percent of today's Christians are saved before the age of fourteen. I'm glad that they are part of the 85 percent! Debbie's and my duty now is to continue to bring our children up in the fear and admonition of the Lord, as well as to prepare for future bedtime discussions with Christina and David. Who knows? It may be during these special times that they, too, acknowledge the Lord Jesus to be their Savior and Lord."

My brother Pete was a year younger than Dave when he came to the Lord. In Pete's words:

We were almost finished building our new cedar home. I hadn't started school yet, being only four years old. Hanging around the house with nothing much to do, I went with my mother to the grocery store. In the car, on the way, I asked my mother to explain to me how Jesus could actually come into my life. I was a small child and interpreted everything literally, so the thought of a grown man crawling inside me was almost impossible to comprehend.

With care and precision my mother explained it simply to me. As we pulled into the parking lot, my mother continued to speak, I listened, and the good news of Jesus became clear. Somewhere between the fruits and the vegetables I prayed to ask Jesus to come into my life.

Still a little surprised that I didn't grow at all (with a grown man inside me), I couldn't wait to tell everyone that Jesus lived in me. On arriving home after shopping, I jumped out of the car and yelled to Haldane, a German man working on our roof, "Haldane, I just asked Jesus into my heart!" He almost fell off the roof with excitement!

Jill:

HELPING YOUR CHILDREN TO BE SURE

Once your children have committed their lives to Christ, it is very important to assure and remind them of the day they heard God speak to them. It's a good idea to encourage them to use Samuel's words, "Speak, Lord, for your servant is listening," whenever they pray. Tell them Samuel's story and point out the similarities to what has occurred in their own lives.

Judy:

There are some problems unique to those who accept Christ as Savior when they are extremely young. When I got older, for example, I wondered whether I really had asked Him into my heart. I remember Mom assuring and reminding me of what I had done when I was four. Even then, I would ask her if she was absolutely sure, or whether I should ask Him into my heart again just to make sure He was there. In response, Mom shared a vivid illustration with me.

She told me to think about a door with locks on the inside. The locks represented different things that we use to keep Christ out of our lives. For some they may represent selfishness, pride, fear, or the like. Christ is knocking on the door of our hearts. Even though He could do so, He won't force open the door and come into our lives unless we unlock the locks. Once the door is unlocked, we open it and let Him walk in.

Now, if some time after we've prayed and asked Jesus into our heart, we have doubts and do it again, nothing will change. He is already inside the door. We need to believe that "if we confess our sins to Him, He can be depended on to forgive us and to cleanse us from every wrong" (1 Jn 1:9, TLB).

Jill:

MOM, THE EVANGELIST OR FISHERPERSON?

Children come to Christ at all hours of the day and night. Samuel came to know God at a very "ordinary" time of day—bedtime. He was just finishing his daily duties and getting ready to curl up for the night.

I've found that's the normal way God comes calling, in the daily doings of life. We must never confine Him to Sunday or Vacation Bible Schools or summer camps. Many children make commitments at these excellent places, but I'm tempted to believe that more hear God calling at home in the course of their everyday, "Nazareth" living.

Evangelism must begin at home. Witnessing is so often thought of as a church activity—perhaps a crusade or an opportunity to do door-to-door evangelism. Yet real evangelism is rather staying in touch with God, fishing rod at the ready. Then, "out of the abundance of the heart, the mouth speaks."

May we take full responsibility to ensure there are abundant things to share about Jesus in our day-to-day Nazareth living. And may we have eyes to see, ears to hear, and tongues ready to tell them how to respond when their time comes.

~

Dig a Little Deeper:

These ideas can be used for further thought and study on your own or in a group.

Some Practical Ideas

1. Go through these verses and get familiar with them yourself. Then pray and expect God to give you an opportunity to use them with someone.

   The fact of sin—Romans 3:23
   The penalty of sin—Romans 6:23
   Jesus died for us—John 3:16
   We must receive Him—Revelation 3:20

   Go through these verses letting the other person read the Scripture for themselves. Ask them if they believe them. Then ask if they would like to pray with you. If they say yes, lead them in a simple prayer of acceptance. Take them back to Revelation 3:20 and point out that the verse says "I will" not "I might" come in. Ask them to pray again and thank God for hearing and answering their prayer.

   If your child is very young when they pray this way, remind them often of the event.

2. A set of resource books designed to teach young children the meaning of the holiness, the omnipresence, omniscience, and omnipotence of God may be useful. Stuart and I wrote *The Danny D* series when we became grandparents and began to try and teach our grandchildren the incommunicable attributes of God. It's hard to teach abstract terms in concrete ways but we believe it can and must be done.

The book that teaches the omnipotence (unlimited power) of God features, among other illustrations, Danny D. wondering why his puppy's tail doesn't fly off when he wags it. "Don't worry, Danny D.," says Papa Stu, "God will hold Prince's tail on, no matter how hard the puppy wags it. God *always* holds everything together!" (This series is published by Baker Books.)

3. Perhaps a simple illustration may help your child to understand the gospel. Read 1 Peter 2:23.

   - Tell the story of the two thieves (picture three crosses).
   - Point out Jesus had never done anything wrong. Look at His cross. It is white and shining.
   - The thieves had done lots of wrong things. Look at their crosses. They are dark.
   - While they were on the cross, one thief asked Jesus to forgive him and take him home to heaven. The other thief didn't want anything to do with Jesus.
   - Look what happened. As soon as he said he was sorry and asked Jesus to forgive him, "Jesus took his sins in His own body on the tree and God punished Him as if He had done all those bad things that they had done."
   - Now the thief that said he was sorry would go to heaven.

   Pray with your child if they would like Jesus to take away their sins.

4. Read Revelation 3:20 with your child.

   Make a door—or draw one. With bolts on the back side and a handle only on the back of the door.

Talk about all the bolts being things we need to unlock so Jesus, who is knocking on our heart's door, can come in.

Some ideas for talking about "bolts":

• We don't want to be good and do what we are told. If Jesus comes into our hearts, He would want us to obey our parents and teachers.

• We don't know how to ask Him in (notice the handle is on the inside). *We* have to open the door. Jesus won't just barge into our lives.

Ask your child if he can think of other reasons he doesn't want to open the door.

If the picture helps, ask your child if they would like to pray a prayer asking the Lord Jesus into their hearts.

Prayer

Pray that God will help you be ready to catch the moments when your child is open to Him.

Pray that God will help you model Christlikeness for your child.

Pray that your child will come to know and love God.

N I N E

My father was a fisherman and I am my father's daughter. But I want to tell you something—fishing is hard work. It's not all sitting in the sunshine on a pier dangling your feet over the edge and having a snooze when nothing's happening. Real fishing takes learning and practicing, walking and wading, casting and hauling, finding the fish and chasing the fish until they take the bait. Once your heavenly Father has taught you His trade you have to have this urge to teach it to your own children. That's good. In fact, that's just how it ought to be!

How to Teach Your Children to Serve

Jill:

ON A MISSIONARY TOUR TO TAIWAN, I was sitting in our bedroom enjoying the only air conditioning in our host's house and listening to happy activity all around. Veteran missionaries Rahn and Stephanie Strickler have five children and run an orderly and efficient family. All the kids have work to do. They earn minimal amounts of money and it is squirreled away for college. All of them know what it is to see poverty, disease, ignorance, and tragedy firsthand. They accompany their parents when they travel to mainland China or visit groups of people who are "without Christ, without God, and without hope" right on their doorstep. All the children are involved practically in the work of the Lord.

They are beautiful children. Their mindset is loving and giving. Beth, their twelve-year-old, served as a waitress for the missionary convention housed on the Christian school grounds to which Stuart and I had come to minister. She worked extraordinarily hard—up at 5:30 A.M., home at 10:00 P.M. At the end of the week she was thrilled to receive $20.00 in tips. Excitedly she told my husband about it. Then she asked him, "Do you need any money?" She would have given it to him in a flash if he had allowed her to! Beth is just a junior high kid, a Samuel, a sweet servant of the Lord learning the joy of serving Jesus and the exhilaration of sacrificial giving.

Some might fault Beth's parents for bringing their children to such a place, for taking some risks, for choosing a very simple lifestyle far from home. But you can't buy what that sweet girl did! Her spontaneous gesture of generosity was worth more than anything money can buy. I was impressed and reminded again of Samuel and his mother, Hannah, and of the saying, "If you would raise a Samuel, be thyself a Hannah." I was thrilled to see this Hannah principle being worked out in this missionary family.

We have more to do with the spiritual blessing of our own children than we ever dream. They will perhaps never serve if we do not serve, never offer a liberal gift of love to another person if we are not spiritually and materially generous. They may never care for the lost if we do not cry out for their souls, and they may never be open to missions if we do not exhibit a missionary mind. If servanthood is a way of life and a top priority for us—a faith focus for the whole family—then it will likely become a way of life for our children.

LEARNING BY DOING

Children learn best by doing, by being involved, by experiment and discovery. Jewish mothers taught their children at home. They used rituals as vivid visual aids. The making of Passover bread was one such example. As mother and children worked together, the mother would explain the significance of what she was doing and the stories behind it all. This way, many lessons would be learned. When Israel celebrated the Feast of Tabernacles, children would take part by cutting down the tree branches used to make booths which were then erected on top of their flat-roofed houses. The families would live in those booths for the duration of the feast. It all had meaning and significance and it was fun! This way the kids learned their nation's history and heard of God's covenant promises.

Children learn by doing. Activity has so much more attraction to a child than passivity.

When we served a youth mission in England in the sixties, all our children were thoroughly and practically involved in our work. When we built our new sanctuary, David, age eight, helped with the manual tasks and earned the same wages as the Bible school students who labored on the project. David also participated in collecting, cutting, and chopping wood for the huge fires at the center, just as young Samuel would have done in his day for the temple fires. Our kids took part in special Christmas programs when the entire neighborhood was invited. One year we poured more than three hundred plaster of paris stands and stuck a candle, Bible verse, and piece of greenery in the wet plaster of each one. Our kids helped make them all. It took all of two days and it was fun. The children knew that what they were doing was for the Lord. They were "ministering before the Lord" under Mother instead of Eli, and they loved every minute of it. Too often our children are bored to death with church things because they are not recruited as Eli's helpers when they are young enough.

A study done on why teens reject Christianity found that:

> Many teenagers believe that there is no place for them in the church. In my study the lack of opportunity for church involvement proved to be the number one reason teens eventually reject religion. Over 75 percent of the youth who demonstrated a general, across-the-board alienation from religion indicated that the church's failure to take them seriously and include them in significant roles is the major cause of their estrangement.[1]

Involvement makes the teenager feel valued and appreciated. I learned that lesson with our three teenagers well before they arrived at the door of adulthood. I insisted they help with summer Vacation Bible School, or in making up games as we filled conference packets, or in putting together Christmas decorations for a Christmas program. They always felt there was something they could do to help. This gave them the good sense that they were on the inside looking out instead of on the outside looking in. That's what involvement does!

Samuel was involved in God's work in all manner of ways. In chapter 3, verse 15, we are told that Samuel "opened the doors of the house of the Lord." He was a doorkeeper. This was a part of the regular duties of a temple servant. It brings to mind Psalm 84 where the writer longs, even faints with desire, to be in God's house. "Better is one day in your courts than a thousand elsewhere," he says. The psalmist describes the joy in joining others in the service of worship. He says he would rather be a doorkeeper in the house of his God than live with the wicked.

As Eli's apprentice, Samuel was the old priest's practical helper in many other ways, as well. Priests had many and varied duties. They would:

offer sacrifices, pronounce benedictions, teach the law, light the lamps in the tabernacle, keep the sacred fire always burning, furnish a quota of wood for the sanctuary, be responsible for the sanctuary itself, act as scribes, supervise tithing, sound trumpets in calling assemblies and in battle, examine lepers, value things given to the tabernacle, act as magistrates, encourage the army on the eve of battle, bear the Ark in battle![2]

While the child Samuel would not be involved in all of these things at every age, he would have learned all these skills before he was grown. First Samuel 2:11 says, "The boy ministered before the Lord under Eli the priest," while 1 Samuel 2:18 says, "Samuel was ministering before the Lord—a boy wearing a linen ephod." The linen ephod was a scanty robe like a tunic worn by inferior priests or apprentices (who nevertheless would do everything the senior men would do).

The point is, Samuel had things to do. From his earliest days he had things to do. This is one way he learned responsibility.

I do not believe a child is ever too young to be given some part in ministering to the Lord. In fact, the sooner they can own a piece of the action, the better. If we wait until we think our kids are responsible before we give them any responsibility, we may wait forever. But if we give them little pieces of their own territory even before they themselves are sure they are ready for it, we may well find them developing into responsible, capable young men and women.

We tried to teach our children that what we do for the Lord is just as important as everything else. Stuart and I have spent our lives up in front of other people. We are visible most of the time, and I was concerned that the children gained the impression that being visible was what serving God was all about.

The apostle Paul was concerned about a similar problem with some of his friends, so he compared each member of the church to a piece of the body. He said that the hidden pieces are vital to the whole body. How could we live without our heart, liver, or veins? Just because someone does their work out of sight, like these organs do, doesn't mean their contribution is unimportant. God's unnoticed servants are just as important as the people on a platform. Probably more so!

The best way I could communicate this principle to my kids was to make sure I was doing lots and lots of behind the scene things. Getting groceries for the old lady down the street and making time for kitchen duty at the youth center (with three hundred guests a week and no dishwasher!) were two things the children could help me with. We tried to teach the kids that just as some people had been given the gift of giving, all Christians were expected to give, so Jesus expected everyone to be helpful, even though not everyone had been given the gift of "helps"!

We tried to explain that the spiritual and practical are equally important. Work is worship and worship is work. In fact, the Hebrew word for "worship" doubles as the word for "work"! Only the specific context determines which translation is appropriate.

Joy comes when our whole being yearns for fellowship with God but especially in corporate worship and in serving God's people in practical ways. Not only should we parents yearn for, seek out, and participate in worship of the Lord for ourselves, we should also yearn for, seek out, and make sure our kids participate in service experiences. There is no age group more vital and open to such opportunities than twelve-year-olds. I believe this is a golden age.

When I first arrived at Elmbrook, our church in Milwaukee, Wisconsin, in 1970, our oldest child, David, was eleven years of age. As he roared into his junior high years, I could see the church needed a program just for his age group. He had lots of friends and we set up a Tuesday evening for them, providing Bible quizzes, games, testimonies, lively music, a search and apply Bible study (a self-discovery method), and prayer exercises of different sorts. I put Dave and four of his friends in charge of the self-discovery Bible time and showed them what to do. They then led their peers into the Bible in bite-sized pieces, asking two basic questions:

1. What does it say?
2. What does it say to *me*?

Other junior high kids (usually I gave the most rambunctious ones the job) led the games and prayer times, and still others prepared refreshments. Adults—a handful only—supervised and advised. Children would prepare dramas and we helped them to give two-minute testimonies to God's working in their lives.

Our program had a rhythm. We made sure that we met once a week for continuity. Then we decided one meeting would major on worship; the next on Bible study and prayer; the next on service to the church, the neighborhood or the needy; and the fourth on outreach and evangelism. It was a surprise to me that by far the most popular week became the one focused on service!

The young people began to bring their friends, and our original group of six grew rapidly. These youngsters had a choice. They could choose extracurricular activities at school, hang around with their pals getting into mischief, or be at "God Squad," as we called it. They chose to come to us. If they had known Psalm 84 they would have told you, "I would rather be a doorkeeper in the house of my God than dwell in the tents of the wicked." Now, many years later, the junior high ministry reaches hundreds of young people a week.

Excitement and activity was plentiful at the temple for Samuel, too. He loved it there. With all their faults, the temple priests—not all of them like Hophni and Phinehas—influenced Samuel for God. *The secret is to employ rather than to entertain.* So often we try to entertain to keep them, rather than employ them—which entertains them and keeps them coming!

SERVE GOD BY SERVING OTHERS

When our junior high youth pastor offered both a summer Christian holiday camp and a work camp down in the inner city, we had a good turnout for the fun and games—but a waiting list for the work camp! The junior high work camp has continued to be the prize camp experience for that age group. There *is* joy in serving Jesus and others for Him, a joy that can *not* be experienced in self-serving or in any other way.

Children of Samuel's age have tender hearts. They may

be self-centered, as we all are, but show them need up close and they put us adults to shame. There would be plenty of need that the boy Samuel would see at the temple. The widow's tears and the leper's grief would be familiar to him. Children have huge hearts for a hurting world. If our children can learn that they are serving the Lord by serving others, they may well integrate the principle into their future careers.

When Dave entered high school we told him (as we told all our children) that out of the three summers he would have before he graduated, one needed to be spent working to contribute to college funds, one would be for family ministry or travel, and one would be his personal choice of Christian service. All our children followed this plan. It was a step of faith, as college is expensive and we needed the money. But because of our family faith focus, we trusted God to supply the college needs, which He did.

Dave chose to join a work team in New Orleans. Fifteen young people went for six weeks of summer vacation with our youth pastor and gave themselves to a New Orleans city mission, working in the French Quarter. They helped poor people in a variety of ways, visited high-rise apartments with the missionaries, ran recreation in the street clubs and led children's camps in the slum areas. They also witnessed to drunks and drug addicts. They slept on the floor of a school building, received $5.00 pocket money a week plus their food... and came home older, wiser, and exhausted. They were, however, full of the joy of the Lord. It was no surprise to us to hear David cite that life-changing, value-forming experience as one of the reasons he is in ministry today.

If our church didn't offer such creative innovative youth adventures, we discovered how we parents could facilitate them. When they did organize such faith adventures, we supported them and made sure our kids were involved in them. We also went along as sponsors whenever we could.

BE CREATIVE AS A FAMILY

The church has no corner on the market regarding creative service ventures. Families can create their own adventures.

Since we decided years ago that our children would breathe in the joy of serving the Lord by serving others, we always tried to have a project going. We'd find something every single one of us could do together. It wasn't easy, but we felt it must be done. As the children grew up, we continued to make family service part of our life.

Many years ago I discovered an old lady who lived quite near us. She was alone, almost blind, and had no one willing to clean her windows. One afternoon I did that, on my own, as a loving gift of Christian service. That day I returned home with a list of things that needed to be done for her. I tried to choose all the things the children could help with. Christians never say, "I don't do windows," because they do them for Him.

Next I brought the old lady's sewing kit home. It was a huge muddle of cotton and buttons, elastic and thimbles. Then I gave it to my six-year-old to tidy up. Dave is my tidy one, so it was an ideal operation for him. I had discovered the lady had grandchildren whose birthdays were coming up. The old lady couldn't get out to buy cards and couldn't afford them, anyway. Judy and David made homemade birthday cards for all of her grandkids and I put them in envelopes, slipped $1.00 in each, and stamped and addressed them for our friend. The kids mailed them.

Then we noticed that the small garden at the front of the old lady's house was an overgrown mess, so we all began to tidy it up. Even my two-and-a-half-year-old helped as we weeded and raked and watered. The next time we went to town, we bought a box of pansies and stopped on the way home to let the children plant them.

Our friend was not a Christian, but each time we left her, she wept. I always asked if we could pray for her. She never refused. So we all held hands and I would ask one of the children to say a prayer asking God to comfort and help her, and then I would close in prayer. It was simple and easy, and oh! what joy it brought to the old lady. But even more, I tell you it brought the joy of Christian service into the lives of David, six, Judy, four, and Pete, two-and-a-half—and of course, their mom.

Look around, find a need. Then set about brainstorming with your family how you can meet that need and choose ways that will involve... everyone.

Judy:

GIVE THEM SOMEONE TO SEE

Some of you may be single mothers and working two jobs and don't have much free time. Or perhaps your time is limited because of other unavoidable circumstances. You are wondering how you can model Christian service for your children.

Take heart! Hannah found herself facing this same situation. Although she was not physically present to model service, she did the next best thing: she found Eli. You can find an Eli, too.

Although Eli had plenty of faults, he was the best person for teaching Samuel about God. Remember, it was Eli who taught Samuel how to minister in the temple (1 Sm

3:1). It was Eli who realized that God was calling Samuel, even though the word of God was rare in those days and visions weren't common (1 Sm 3:1). It was Eli who insisted that Samuel tell him what God had said the night before, and it was Eli who accepted his punishment, understanding that God would do what was right and good (1 Sm 3:18). Believe it or not, Eli taught Samuel quite a bit about loving and serving God!

When we look for role models for our children, we often try to find perfect people. Unfortunately, we're always going to be disappointed. We need to look for the best person around who can teach our children about Jesus. How do you define best? A person whom God is using to change lives. Those who display many of the qualities and characteristics of Christlike character are described in Galatians 5. They serve God with all of their heart, soul, and mind, despite imperfections. These are the people with whom I want my children to rub shoulders.

When we lived in England and my parents worked with the youth mission, teenagers from the four corners of the globe came to be involved in Bible school or house parties. My brothers and I grew up with plenty of role models—kids who loved the Lord and were studying to know Him better.

My older brother, David, loved tools and building. When my dad and some of the men from the youth mission decided to build our house, Dave wanted to help. The carpenter, Haldane, took Dave under his wing and Dave worked alongside him.

David noticed the difference in Haldane's work ethic, which my brother compared with that of the unbelievers working on the project. When one of the men hit his hand with a hammer, he turned the air blue. When the same day Haldane fell from a ladder and landed on some sharp building implements, cutting himself, he grimaced and made some loud noises, but didn't take the Lord's name in vain. Haldane always worked hard to do the best job possible, whereas some others would clock off early if the foreman wasn't around. Haldane would let David know that the Lord expected us to do our very best, whoever was watching. God was always watching, he told my brother. And David listened to him, watched him, and mimicked him. Haldane was a great role model.

As my brothers have grown older, many people have asked us what it was like growing up as pastor's kids. I feel one of the benefits of belonging to a family in the ministry is being surrounded by God's people, people who day after day love the Lord and give up everything in their lives to serve him.

I will never forget meeting Corrie ten Boom and hearing stories of her ghastly experiences in the concentration camps. I remember even more clearly her discussions about her love for the Lord and her strong faith in Jesus. Even though she went through terrible ordeals, she never gave up believing that God had a plan and that He was in complete control. This made an impression on me at the age of fourteen. Expose your kids to people who serve the Lord, and they will begin to develop a hunger for doing likewise.

But that's not all. The example of parents and other influential people who are serving the Lord may have a restraining influence on our children's actions. As my brother, Peter, puts it:

The quiet, strong presence of my father and the tender, caring love of my mother were a restraining influence in my life. As I grew in stature, my parents grew in reputation. As they grew in reputation, my respect for them also grew.

I remember hearing of a famous pastor's son who had "gone off the deep end." The pastor resigned to spend more time with the boy and his ministry was cut off. I told myself, as a thirteen-year-old, that I would never allow myself to destroy my parents' ministry. I remember thinking in times of temptation, *What effect could this have on my mom or my dad?* I made decisions based on my answer.

GIVE THEM A CHANCE TO STRETCH

Allowing our children the opportunity to "do" and "see" will give them the chance to grow in their Christian life. First Samuel 2:26 describes the boy Samuel growing in favor with God and with men. It's not always easy for us to see our children developing at a rapid rate, however. We may like them to grow a little, but we may not be ready for a lot of stretching.

This may be especially true for mothers. When our kids reach the teen years and they are trying to find out who they are, many require autonomy from us in order to accomplish this. Unfortunately, this is often a time in a mother's development when she is doing some soul-searching of her own. She is trying to figure out what she is going to do with the rest of her life and what she has done with her life so far. Her children are a big part of her accomplishments. So, sometimes we see a tug of war with mom trying to hold on to her children and the kids trying to gain some independence.

We mothers must try to allow our children to grow and stretch. One of the ways we can help them do this is to trust them before they prove themselves trustworthy. I have had to do this with my three-year-old. He is trying to become independent, and sometimes I find myself wanting to slow down the clock. For his third birthday, he received a two-wheeler bike with training wheels. He took to this bike like a duck to water. Within minutes, he was racing up and down the sidewalk of our block.

Drew has been good about not going on the street when he is outside playing, but before now I never had to deal with this issue when he rode his bike. My stomach churned as I pushed Jordan in the stroller, trying to catch up with Drew before he reached the street. I trusted him and yet he was only three. Thank the Lord, he stopped and waited for me.

Mom has told me that this idea of trusting people before they prove trustworthy continues throughout parenting. When I was a teenager, I was dating someone who did not at all meet with my mother's approval. One evening, I came in after a date and said to her that we needed to talk about the situation. We went into her bedroom and I asked her whether she trusted me. She said that she did trust me—it was other people's children that she wasn't so sure about! I replied that she would have to let me go, and together we would have to pray that all my mistakes would be small ones.

Now, this was not Mom's original prayer. She had been praying, "No mistakes." And yet, that isn't really fair, is it? Our parents made mistakes and so did we; we can't expect our children not to make them. The problem is that the ramifications of mistakes in this day can be deadly. In effect, Mom had to trust me before I was trustworthy. And she did.

Before Samuel had proved his trustworthiness, God Himself entrusted to the lad some crucial news for Eli. The first thing God asked Samuel to do was extremely difficult. Samuel had to go to the man who in effect had reared him and tell him that all his descendants would die when they were in the prime of their lives (1 Sm 2:33); both of his sons would die on the same day (1 Sm 2:34); and another priest would take the place of Eli's family (1 Sm 2:35-36). The news was so devastating that Samuel didn't want to tell Eli (1 Sm 3:15). Yet, he did what God wanted him to do and told the old priest.

God provided Samuel with an opportunity to stretch his faith—a chance for the boy to realize that God's will was paramount and that he was a servant of the Lord. Samuel's simple act of obedience proved God's trust and led to a lifetime of opportunities to tell others the words of the Lord.

Jill:
A NEW TWIST ON AN OLD VERSE

One final thought. The much quoted verse in the book of Proverbs, "Train a child in the way he should go and when he is old he will not turn from it" (Prv 22:6), was given a new twist for me as I listened to a radio preacher expound upon it. He explained it really meant, "Train a child in the way *he* should go, not the way *you* think he should go!" He said it could be translated, "Train a child according to his 'bent,' according to the way God has made him."

This is important. It is reasonable to assume that if God has given our children particular gifts (and He has), then He has a particular place for those gifts to be used within the local body. It may be in a lay capacity or it may be in vocational Christian work, but God has a specific place in mind for those gifts to be used.

I think particularly of Peter and his athletic abilities. When he was in college, we pointed out Christian avenues of service in athletics. This resulted in Peter playing on a missionary sports team, first in the Philippines and then in South America. The team worked in conjunction with the local church or missionary, packed the local stadium with local people, played a local team, and preached at halftime! It was on one of these tours that Peter says he was called to ministry.

Taking the time and trouble to find matching avenues of service for our children's gifting can light a spark of enthusiastic service that will last for a lifetime. And it avoids trying to put round pegs in square holes!

A FINAL CHALLENGE

As parents who have found great freedom and joy in serving Jesus, Stuart and I have discovered the apple doesn't fall too far from the tree. The greatest motivation possible for a child to grow up loving and serving God is to watch a mom and dad who spend their days loving and serving God.

Hannah began training Samuel when he was a baby. From the moment he took his first breath, Christian worship and service was in the very air that filled his lungs. Little wonder we find him growing up "doing" worship and service and being thoroughly involved in the work of God. It was largely because of a loving, godly mother that Samuel grew up to become a wonderful and godly young man.

"If you would raise a Samuel, be thyself a Hannah." It's a choice all of us need to make. It's a choice that leads to indescribable joy. And it's a choice you'll never regret.

Just ask Hannah!

~

Dig a Little Deeper:

These ideas can be used for further thought and study on your own or in a group.

Discuss

Lest we have left the impression that service has only to do with spiritual exercises, we would like to point out that bringing up children to serve involves secular and practical activities, too. When the Bible says the child Samuel ministered before the Lord (1 Sm 2:11-18) we have already pointed out this work of ministering included very mundane duties. Most of the things Samuel did for Eli were "helping" duties. If our kids can be a help to Mom by cleaning up their rooms, setting the table, or taking the dog for a walk, they need to learn to see that as ministering to the Lord. Pleasing our parents pleases God.

1. Read Luke 2:52 and 1 Samuel 2:26 and talk about the similarities between Jesus and Samuel.

   What do you think it means to grow in:
   Wisdom?
   Stature?
   Favor with God?
   Favor with man?

   How can growing in all these areas contribute to our future service for the Lord?

2. Jesus served the Lord as surely as Samuel did. But his upbringing was very different. In fact, the only time we read about Jesus doing something that was spiritual or "religious" apart from things with His family on the Sabbath, He got into trouble from His parents!

Read Luke 2:41-52. What does this tell you about Jesus' spiritual awareness at twelve years of age?

What does His parents' reaction teach us?

What about the teachers of the Law who listened to and answered Jesus' questions? What does that say to us?

Read Luke 2:51. What does this verse teach us about children serving God?

Some Practical Ideas

1. Plan a vacation with a difference.

   - Choose a church or mission for your family to help (ask your pastor).
     Inner-city church
     Building project
     Evangelism or children's work
     Relief or refugee organization

   - Put aside two weeks. One week isn't quite long enough.

   - Challenge your youth group to stretch and to commit to do something for others, rather than themselves.

   - Ask for a commitment from oldest to youngest to read the Bible and pray for ten minutes every day of the work camp.

2. Each Christmas, along with the cards, our family receives photographs of people who are serving the Lord. Some may be pastors, others are missionaries. Some photos are of families in the secular world who are serving God in their local churches. These Christ-

mas family photos are put in a photo album and updated each year. At breakfast time we take that album and remind ourselves of all our friends around the world. We pray for a few each day. It really helps to have their faces smiling at us. We trust it helps them in that ministry, too. This is one way you can involve your children in praying for people who are serving the Lord. Such intercession can also raise their awareness of world missions.

3. Another breakfast prayer time idea is to subscribe to a missionary magazine. This focuses interest on a specific project in a certain area. Read a paragraph of information every day and get one of the children to pray for the needs of a Christian worker. This can give the children a world view and turn their attention to the need for God's servants to work for Him.

Prayer

Pray for your children to come to Christ and develop a desire to serve Him.

Pray for the Christian mentors at school or church who influence your children.

Pray that your own parenting may model a happy and satisfying service for the Lord.

Pray about 1 Samuel 2:21 every day for your child. "The boy Samuel grew up in the presence of the LORD."

Epilogue

~

SOMEONE HAS SAID, it's not how we begin the Christian life that matters, but how we end it. How do we finish strong?

How did Samuel turn out? Very well indeed, it seems to me. There is no record of any lapse in his continued walk with the Lord. Rather we learn that the whole country heard about his touch with God and his authority as prophet and priest (1 Sm 3:20). The Israelites were excited because the Word of God was given regularly to the people after such a long dry period in their history.

Can you imagine Hannah and Elkanah's pride as their son became a popular and respected leader? Samuel began to travel on a circuit of the entire country, always arriving back home in Ramah (1 Sm 7:15-17). I like that. He always came home! Hannah and Elkanah weren't perfect parents, but they did enough things right. There is no way of making sure your children, no matter how well you model, pray, and practice these principles and ideas, will "make it" spiritually. But we can give it our best spiritual shot and then leave the rest to Him.

Perhaps this book has frustrated you because your opportunity has passed—your children are long gone or you are estranged from them. If so, remember that we must influence those we can, reiterate age-old values, the absolutes of Scripture, and the way of the Lord. We can teach Sunday School, open our homes and hearts to encourage single parents, counsel or listen to hurting friends and neighbors, or tell others about available resources. All of us can still help to strengthen the family. As we catch our little, big fish or help others haul them in, we will sense we are involved in something bigger than ourselves. Something close to the heart of God.

A few weeks ago I was sitting on a plane next to an eight-year-old. He was "between" parents, on the way from his mother to his father. He was surrounded by eight-year-old paraphernalia to keep him occupied. I wondered who he belonged to—how he was coping with going to and fro between two different caregivers who lived on opposite sides of the country. We talked a little—he was a really neat kid. On the surface he didn't appear to be bothered by his experience. He seemed well cared for. Suddenly I had a thought: *Has anyone cared for his soul?* I looked with new insight at my small companion. He was the same age as our oldest grandson. I thought about Danny. He had believing grandparents on both sides of the family, pastors as uncles, and a host of Sunday School teachers looking after him—not to mention his own mom and dad intent on helping him fall in love with Jesus. I had no way of knowing the circumstances surrounding that little guy next to me, but he didn't appear to have much Christian input into his life.

I was tired and wanted to sleep. I don't know why it is that the fish are usually biting when you are too tired to raise your rod, but I asked the Lord to help me and we went fishing.

Look around you. Be a Christian mother, grandmother, sister, or aunt to a world of lost people swimming in a sea of confusion. There is no greater joy.

I think of a friend I have who is single. She has served the Lord and children all her life. Her footprints are all over the Christian life experience of thousands of young people. She would love to have been married, but in God's economy it just never happened. She would have made a marvelous mother. One day as we talked about this, she told me the Lord "had" given her children of all ages and nationalities. Hundreds of them. Then she showed me this verse: "More are the children of the barren woman than of her who has a husband" (Is 54:1). "It's true in my case, Jill," she said cheerfully. "God has given me so many marvelous kids. I have never been bored or dull. My job as a spiritual mother is to bring them to Christ and to keep them Christian!"

I believe that is the job God wants every one of us— with or without children—involved in for the rest of our lives. The next time when friends knock on the door and ask us to come out and play, I pray they will find a notice hung on our gate: "Sorry—gone fishing."

~

Appendix:
Starting a Support Group

~

Prior to beginning the process of developing a support group, accept the fact that during times of crisis it may seem easier to isolate yourself than to reach out for help and support from others. Keep in mind that in times of crisis our emotions are more intense and can lead us to believe that we are alone, without understanding, and without a soul in the world who cares about our situation. Learn to be honest about such thoughts and feelings, but make a decision not to act on them. Continue to reach out to receive the help God offers through His people, even if it is the last thing in the world you feel like doing.

Begin small. It is unrealistic to expect to find a lot of people who will instantly become your support group. A good group takes time to develop. Begin by praying for and thinking of perhaps one person who you sense is trustworthy, compassionate, an empathetic listener, and utilizes godly wisdom. It is not necessary that you know this person well, but it is necessary that this be a person you believe you can trust. When you think of such a person, contact her and ask if you can meet with her to talk about what you are experiencing.

As you meet with this individual, let her know that you

need and desire ongoing support. Ask her if she knows of other people who have experienced or are experiencing a similar situation. From this point begin developing a list of others who may be interested in becoming part of a support group.

Although it seems risky and you may feel foolish, begin contacting the individuals on the list you developed. Be honest with them about your struggles but do not demand their involvement in a support group. Simply let them know what you need and ask them if they would be interested in becoming involved. Often people will be extremely appreciative of your contact with them and will communicate that they need the support as much as you do.

All it takes to form a support group is more than one person. Do not be discouraged if you only find a few people who can be part of the support group you wish to form. Begin with the people who are interested and schedule your first meeting. This first meeting should be a time of getting to know each other but also a time to decide on and formulate the purposes and goals of the group. Put your purposes and goals on paper and make sure that each person receives a copy. This will help the group to stay on task as you grow together. In addition, be certain the individuals in your group agree to rules concerning confidentiality and commitment as standards for meeting together.

Remember that developing an effective support group takes time. During the time it takes to organize a group, be certain to continue to reach out for help and support rather than withdrawing and isolating.*

~

* This was written by Jenny Hickman, a staff member of Elmbrook Church.

Notes

~

TWO

A God-Centered Focus

1. Russell Chandler, *Racing toward 2001* (Grand Rapids, Mich.: Zondervan, 1992), 92.
2. Chandler, 92.
3. W. Brueggeman, *Interpretation: A Bible Commentary for Teaching* (Louisville, Ken.: John Knox, 1990), 10.
4. *New Bible Dictionary,* 2nd Edition, edited by J.D. Douglas and N. Hillyer (Wheaton, Ill.: Tyndale, 1982), 125.
5. Robert Gordon, *First and Second Samuel* (Grand Rapids, Mich.: Zondervan, 1986), 71 ff.
6. "Things," text by special permission of River Oaks Music Company and BMG Music of Beverly Hills, California.

FIVE

A Mother's Prayer Life

1. This was taken from a talk on prayer which I heard S.D. Gorden give.

SIX

Let It Out, Let It In, Let It Go

1. Elisabeth Elliot, quoted in *Lord, If I Ever Needed You, It's Now* by Creath Davis (Grand Rapids, Mich.: Baker).

2. Mrs. Charles Cowman, *Streams in the Desert* (Grand Rapids, Mich.: Zondervan, 1965), 143.

SEVEN
Keep Them Near the Ark

1. These ideas were adapted from: Barbara Newman and Philip Newman, *Development through Life: A Psychological Approach,* 5th edition (Pacific Grove, Cal.: Brook/Cole, 1991).
2. These ideas were adapted from: R. Muuss, *Theories of Adolescence,* 5th edition (New York: Random House, 1988).

EIGHT
Leading Your Child to Christ

1. Hall, *New Directions for Children's Ministries* (Kansas City, Mo.: Beacon Hill, 1980).
2. Marjorie Soderholm, *Understanding the Pupil Part II: The Primary and Junior Child* (Grand Rapids, Mich.: Baker, 1975), 45.

NINE
How to Teach Your Children to Serve

1. Dr. Robert Laurent, *Keeping Your Child in Touch with God* (Elgin, Ill.: David C. Cook, 1988), 23.
2. Orville J. Nave, *Nave's Topical Bible* (Chicago, Ill.: Moody, 1975), 1006.

Other Books of Interest from Servant Publications

A House of Many Blessings
A Christian Guide to Hospitality
Quin Sherrer and Laura Watson

Christian homes can provide comfort, healing, friendship, rest, and encouragement to all who enter them. Quin Sherrer and Laura Watson give readers a vision of the tremendous value of ordinary, down-home, Christian hospitality. A creative, practical, and inspiring guide to opening one's home to friends, extended family, fellow Christians, and those in need. *$8.99*

Grandparenting
The Agony and the Ecstacy
Jay Kesler

Godly grandparents can make a difference in the lives of grandchildren who are often confused and bewildered by the world in which they live. Here is a book to encourage, equip, and motivate Christian grandparents, no matter what their circumstances. *$8.99*

Conspiracy of Kindness
*A Refreshing New Approach to Sharing
the Love of Jesus with Others*
Steve Sjogren

"The conspiracy of kindness" operates on a very simple premise: that God is passionately in love with unbelievers and can win them most effectively through simple acts of kindness. These acts of love are very easy and practical, requiring no training. They can be accomplished by everyone.

If you are burned out on evangelism, if sharing the gospel doesn't seem to be your gift, join the ranks of those who are best-suited for becoming secret agents of God's love. *$8.99*

Available at your Christian bookstore or from:
**Servant Publications • Dept. 209 • P.O. Box 7455
Ann Arbor, Michigan 48107**
Please include payment plus $2.75 per book
for postage and handling.
*Send for our FREE catalog of Christian
book, music, and cassettes.*